AMERICAN SOLVENCY

AMERICAN SOLVENCY

One Constitutional Amendment

to Permanently Fix

Much of What is Broken

in American Government

Wes Nicholson

Squaring the Circle
Portland, Oregon

Squaring The Circle LLC
Portland, Oregon

Cover design by Roy Migabon
www.roymigabon.co.cc

Publisher's Cataloging-in-Publication (Provided by Quality Books, Inc.)

Nicholson, Wes.
American solvency : one constitutional amendment to permanently fix much of what is broken in American government / [Wes Nicholson].
p. cm.
LCCN 2011933412
ISBN-13: 978-0983790808
ISBN-10: 0983790809

1. Debts, Public--United States. 2. Constitutional amendments--United States. I. Title.

HJ8119.N53 2012 336.3'4'0973
QBI11-600133

EDB 9 CA 75

Printing information for this book may be found on the last page

For Pamela, with all my love

Contents

• 1 •
THE DANGER

Some innocents 'scape not the thunderbolt.
– Shakespeare, *Antony and Cleopatra*

DO YOU REMEMBER the innocence of childhood? Maybe you recall a time when life's burdens did not yet weigh upon your shoulders. Perhaps you remember a blissfully ignorant moment when your greatest anxiety was over the first day of school. Greater concerns, no doubt, existed—dangers, even—but your parents shielded you from them. By sheltering children from want and from danger, parents preserve and prolong an innocence that is one of life's blessings. Later, as we leave our childhoods behind, the things we were shielded from become clear, and the duty to shield the next generation from those things passes on to us.

As with life, citizenship within a society begins in innocence. Do you remember what we first learned about American government? We learned about the British Empire, the Thirteen Colonies, taxation without representation, and the Founding Fathers. We learned about Life, Liberty, and the pursuit of Happiness, the Declaration of Independence, and the Revolutionary War. We learned about "We The People," the Constitution, the separation of powers, and checks and balances. We learned about freedom, democracy, justice, and equality. This simplified history and these simple ideals are the root of citizenship in America. They are the beginning of the explanation of American government, and in the beginning, they are all the explanation we need.

Like the innocence of childhood, however, the innocence of citizenship does not last forever. Reality intrudes and complicates things. Liberty is in tension with both equality and security. Our republican form of government is not a pure democracy. The constraints placed upon government to guard against tyranny also reduce governmental efficiency. It is not possible to be perfectly devoted at the same time to every principle worth defending, and in practice we must often settle for trade-offs struck between our principles.

At the moment, reality is complicating things in a frightening way. People of every political persuasion agree that America has a debt problem that is reaching crisis proportions. Words like "bankrupt" and "broke" are beginning to be used to describe our future.

Although our latest recession did not cause these problems, it has accelerated them. Our debts are growing faster than our ability to repay them. Alarming financial conditions that once seemed decades away now appear disturbingly close. America is heading toward insolvency.

We could choose to ignore the threat of insolvency. We could decide to just keep our heads down and hope that some way, somehow, everything will turn out for the best. After all, we regularly see low turnouts at election time and the country still seems to be here.

More often than not, it isn't crucial for us to pay deep attention to political matters. In other places in the world, politics can literally be a matter of life and death in a way that is just not the case in the United States. Here, no matter which way our votes go, the outcomes are basically tolerable, and we seem to muddle through. Indeed, this is one of the blessings of liberty in America: We can flourish even under an innocent citizenship.

The consequences of insolvency, however, will be disastrous, and careless innocence alone will not save us from them. Whether we like it or not, the hard reality of our nation's long-term financial situation is calling upon us to rouse ourselves from innocence and shoulder the burdens of a more mature citizenship.

Our country is in peril. The duty to protect it—and to secure its blessings, to ourselves and our posterity—has passed to us.

The danger we must defend against is not yet at our door, but it has reached the shadows across the street. And it is coming.

· 2 ·
WHAT HAPPENED?

AMERICA HAS a long-term debt problem. Every year, our government spends more money than it receives. The difference between the two—the deficit—is financed by taking out debt. Our debt increases as the years go by. If the debt gets large enough, America will be unable to service it and will become insolvent.

We know these things. Yet even though the risks have lately become far more apparent, our deficit spending seems to be firmly entrenched. Financially, our country is like an airplane on autopilot, headed toward a mountain-side.

We can hardly hope to find a solution to our problem without first understanding what has caused it. As it turns out, our ruinous financial situation can be explained by a few underlying factors.

2.1 Getting In

WATER FLOWS DOWNHILL, following the path of least resistance. Societies tend to follow paths of least resistance, too.

In establishing spending policies and policies that impact our revenues, our society could follow one of two paths. On one path, we could constrain ourselves to consider our finances in total, so that the money we spend is no more than the money we receive. On the other path, we could consider our policies piece-meal, meaning separately and individually. Between the two, setting policies piece-meal has proven to be the path of least resistance.

Consider how we typically approach policies on the spending side. When our government first decides to spend money toward a particular purpose, it tends not to consider the amount it would like to spend for that purpose as a portion of a limited amount, such as the total amount of money that will be available to spend for the year. Instead, it tends to consider how much would be desirable to spend toward that purpose in and of itself.

Our government would have to expend extra effort to keep its overall finances in mind when considering additional spending toward any one purpose. The House of Representatives, the Senate, and the President would have to coordinate among themselves politically to make sure that additional spending would not require deficit spending (or increased deficit spending).

Nothing forces our government spend that extra effort. Since spending that extra effort would be harder to do, our government ends up separately approving spending toward various purposes without ensuring that our total spending toward all purposes is within our means.

Moreover, when considered separately and individually, each purpose for which our government spends money for the most part sounds like a good thing to spend money on—and if it sounds like a good thing to spend money on, it surely also sounds like a good thing to spend more money on. Under our political process, the amount of money spent for any particular purpose tends to be determined by things like the amount of money spent previously for that purpose, or the effectiveness of lobbying and advocacy for that purpose, as opposed to the portion of the money available for us to spend that we believe should be spent for that purpose.

Consider two hypothetical citizens, Citizen A and Citizen B. Each citizen has preferences regarding the priority of the various purposes toward which government spends money. Citizen A would prefer that government prioritize health care, and would prefer that government spend more on health care than it currently does. Citizen B, on the other hand, would prefer that government prioritize and spend more on national defense than it currently does.

Clearly, the preferences of Citizen A and Citizen B are in tension with each other. Nobody likes tension. Tension causes bad feelings. Elected officials don't like to cause bad feelings among their constituents, since bad feelings may hurt their chances for continued employment.

So, since nothing forces our government to think about the impact of individual spending decisions on our overall spending, it tends to avoid directly addressing the tension. Instead, when there is sufficient political support to increase health care spending, our government will increase health care spending in order to satisfy Citizen A. Similarly, when there is sufficient political support for increased spending on national defense, our government will increase spending on national defense in order to satisfy Citizen B.

Citizen A does want more money to be spent toward health care. However, Citizen A almost certainly does not want our government to spend more money on health care if it means that our government will be spending more money overall than it expects to bring in. In other words, Citizen A wants more money spent on health care, but not at the expense of a balanced budget. Similarly, Citizen B wants more money spent on national defense, but not at the expense of a balanced budget.

In reality, both Citizen A and Citizen B want a balanced budget, and each wants more money to be spent on the purpose they prefer. However, instead of addressing the inherent tension between those competing preferences, our government ends up increasing the amount of money spent on both purposes and taking the budget out of balance to do so. As a result, although both Citizen A's preferences and Citizen B's preferences have seemingly been addressed, neither Citizen A nor Citizen B got what they really wanted. Neither Citizen's preference is truly satisfied.

In practice, our government approves of spending based upon what it has sufficient political support to enact one piece at a time. It seldom, if ever, approves of spending based upon what it can financially afford to spend in total. As a result, spending policies are established to address the priorities of isolated segments of the electorate, one at a time, regardless of the effect on spending as a whole.

Since our government is not forced to spend the money at its disposal as if it were a limited resource, our demands for government spending tend to become unbounded. When considered piece-meal, there is no limit to the things that would be good to spend money on, or to increase spending on. What arises resembles an ever-open maw, always fed but never satisfied, endlessly moaning "*More!*"

We approach policies on the revenue side in this way, too, such as our policies regarding taxation and regulation of commerce. As with establishing spending policies, we tend not to debate the total impact of our policies upon revenue and instead consider such policies piece-meal. That is, we ask whether an individual policy—cutting taxes, for example—sounds like a good idea in and of itself. As with our spending policies, we do this at least in part because nothing forces us to do otherwise. As a result, policies that impact our government's revenue also end up being individually approved without fully considering our overall finances.

Since our government is not forced to consider the overall consequences to the budget of spending policies and revenue-impacting policies, establishing such policies piece-meal is easier than establishing them with an eye to their total impact. The first factor underlying our long-term debt problem is simply that *it is easier for us to get into deficit spending than it is for us to stay out.* Between the two, getting into deficit spending is the path of least resistance.

2.2 Staying In

ONCE WE HAVE STARTED to spend in deficit, our society could follow one of two paths. On one path, we could balance our budgets in order to stop our deficit spending. On the other path, instead of balancing our budgets, we could continue spending in deficit. Between the two, continuing our deficit spending has proven to be the path of least resistance.

Balancing any government's budget is inherently hard. Consider how we approach the prospect of cutting spending. In a hypothetical question commonly posed in civics classes and in news articles, students (or readers) are given a list of the various purposes for which our government spends money along with the amounts of money spent for each purpose. In such hypothetical questions, the total money spent toward all purposes is more than the amount of money that our government takes in (a very real and all too common scenario).

The students (or readers) are then challenged to balance our government's budget. For what purposes should less money be spent, and by how much? For what purposes should more money be spent, if any?

Some people who have preconceived ideological or partisan preferences might find balancing our government's budget to be easy. However, most of the purposes for which our government spends money are, generally speaking, good things. Indeed, for each of our government's spending programs, there must have been enough people who saw merit in that spending at the time it was established that the average citizen today is likely to see at least some merit in that spending, too. As a result, most people would see most of the things we spend money on as good things to spend money on, and most people therefore find it hard to even hypothetically balance our government's budget.

Making matters worse, to be of any practical value, a balanced budget proposal would have to be acceptable to enough citizens that it could actually be enacted. Proposals that may be acceptable to some citizens will almost certainly be unacceptable to others, and bringing a governmental budget into balance to the complete satisfaction of everybody is inherently impossible. Yet without sufficient political support, no hypothetical balanced budget can be enacted.

The House, the Senate, and the President must politically coordinate to bring our government out of deficit spending. The problem of balancing the budget, which is difficult enough for any one person to resolve to their own satisfaction, becomes that much more difficult when it must additionally be resolved to the satisfaction of such a wide range of interested parties. This makes it hard to come up with any balanced budget proposal.

Not only that, we must deal with some fundamentally different types of spending in attempting to balance our budgets. Some types of spending cannot be avoided by passing new laws. When our government enters into a contract, for example, it cannot avoid that spending by just passing a law to nullify its contractual obligations. It must either satisfy the terms of the contract or else breach the contract and abide by whatever remedy a court may impose on it.

In particular, the interest payments required to service our national debt cannot be avoided by passing laws to eliminate those obligations. Our government cannot get out of servicing its debt just by passing a law declaring that its debt doesn't exist.

So, in balancing our budgets, some of our spending is unavoidable. We will remain obligated to such spending no matter how much we may debate our budget and no matter what we may ultimately decide.

Other types of spending are avoidable, though. One type of avoidable spending that our government engages in is *discretionary spending*, so called because the *currently-sitting government* (that is, the people currently elected to represent us in our legislative and executive branches) has discretion in spending that money however it chooses. Another type of avoidable spending that our government engages in is *mandatory spending*, under which *previously-sitting governments* (that is, the people who had been elected to represent us in past years) committed the country, by law, to spend money for various purposes in future years. Mandatory spending includes those spending programs often referred to as *entitlements*.

Both of these types of spending can be avoided by passing new laws. Just because a spending program has been enacted does not mean that it needs to continue, or that it needs to continue with the same funding.

However, both discretionary and mandatory spending tend to exhibit a "ratchet effect," a political inertia that makes it difficult to decrease levels of funding from one year to the next. Once our government begins spending money for any particular purpose, beneficiaries of that money can be identified. Those beneficiaries then become symbols of the benefits of that spending—and, by implication, of the cruelty of reducing or ending it.

This ratchet effect is particularly problematic for mandatory spending programs. On top of the political inertia common to both types of spending programs, mandatory spending programs establish legally binding commitments for our government to spend money in future years. Once established, these commitments continue to exist until altered by new laws.

Advocates of discretionary spending programs must summon enough political support to commit our government to the levels of spending they desire. In contrast, advocates of mandatory spending programs need only summon sufficient political support to thwart efforts to change the levels of spending that our government is already committed to. The type of political coordination required to reduce discretionary spending is therefore very different in nature from the type of political coordination required to reduce mandatory spending.

As with our spending policies, our revenue-impacting policies can also be hard to change once established. For example, it is hard to raise taxes in an attempt to increase government revenue. Any specific tax increase will fall on particular people. Those people are not likely to welcome the additional burden and will struggle to prevent it. Like proposals to reduce spending, proposals aimed at increasing revenue may also fail due to lack of support.

The piece-meal policy-making that has led to our deficits has allowed us to avoid political tension and hide from hard choices. Our entrenched deficits are thus the result of conflict avoidance. To end our deficit spending, we would have to address the tensions between our policies—but that is no easier to do when trying to get out of deficit spending than it was to do when trying to stay out. Whether we consider remedies on the spending side or remedies on the revenue side, bringing an out-of-balance budget back into balance is inherently difficult.

It is easier to just keep our spending-side and revenue-side programs in place in their current forms and take on additional debt to do so. The second factor underlying our long-term debt problem is simply that *it is easier for us to stay in deficit spending than it is for us to get out.* Between the two, staying in deficit spending is the path of least resistance.

Our entrenched deficit spending has not been intentional, though. Getting into deficit spending, and continuing to spend in deficit once we have started, are merely paths of least resistance. Ultimately, we have set course for the mountain and engaged the autopilot not because we intended to, but because it was the easiest thing to do.

2.3 A Side Effect: Poisonous Illusions

IN ADDITION TO the role they play in directly causing our deficits, the getting-in factor and staying-in factor have had a perverse side effect. By allowing us to avoid the inherent tensions between our divergent policy preferences, they have fostered poisonous illusions about the sorts of policies that are politically possible in this country.

Consider the simplistic model in which the world of politics is represented as a spectrum along a line. In matters of spending, people on one side of the political spectrum tend to prefer larger spending programs and more extensive taxes. In contrast, people on the other side of the political spectrum tend to prefer smaller spending programs and less extensive taxes.

Furthermore, some people on each side of the spectrum are especially ideological, or partisan. On one side, some people believe that if only governmental programs were more robust, and if only taxation were increased to some necessary corresponding level, a socialist utopia would arise, and the country would be a much better place. On the other side, some people believe that if only government would stop draining resources from citizens and get out of the way, a capitalist utopia would arise, and the country would be a much better place.

Neither of these competing sets of policy preferences has a chance of being enacted into law in its entirety. However, due to our piece-meal decision making process, policies from each set of preferences—a spending program here, a tax cut there—are enacted from time to time. Because such policies are hard to end once begun, they may then prove to be enduring.

Out of this, the poisonous illusions appear. Experiencing some success in moving toward their own utopian vision reinforces the faith of partisans on each side of the spectrum in the degree of political support for their own preferred policies. Both by beginning and by enduring, various policies become evidence to political partisans of the potential to achieve their entire policy vision.

However, the scraps of these competing visions that manage to survive piece-meal evaluation and become actual policy do not reflect an acceptance among the electorate of either policy vision as a whole. There are still enough voters on each side of the political spectrum to prevent the full policy vision of the other side from being implemented.

But deficit spending shields partisans on each side of the political spectrum from understanding that neither policy vision has sufficient support to be fully realized. Thereafter, heedless of political realities, each side adheres to policy demands that can never be achieved.

In response to our entrenched deficits, for example, the impulse on one side of the political spectrum seems to be that our problem is basically a revenue problem: Our government's revenues are not high enough. Accordingly, the solution is to raise taxes in order to increase our government's revenues and close the deficit. The impulse on the other side of the political spectrum seems to be that our problem is basically a spending problem: Our government is spending too much money. Accordingly, the solution is for our government to spend less money in order to close the deficit.

In the ensuing political clash, each side comes armed with evidence of the successful partial fulfillment of its own vision: the country seems to want various spending programs; the country seems to want low taxes. This evidence causes each side to operate under the illusion that its entire policy vision has greater support among the electorate than it actually does.

On the basis of this illusory evidence, each side feels less inclined to compromise in order to end our deficit spending. The poisonous illusions thereby make the political coordination that might end our deficits that much harder. So, in a vicious cycle, we find ourselves unable to avoid deficit spending; our deficits foster illusions about the political potential of utopian visions; and those illusions then poison the well with respect to any potential solutions that may offend those utopian visions.

By never fully coming to terms with political realities, each side becomes blinded by a bright future shimmering just across the sands, a future that cannot and will not come: *"Our country's troubles could all be solved! If only... If only..."*

2.4 A Violation of Fundamental Principles

MAKING DECISIONS regarding spending-side and revenue-side policies in a piece-meal way is relatively easy, which has led us into deficit spending. Balancing our budgets is relatively hard, which has kept us spending in deficit.

The getting-in factor and the staying-in factor explain a great deal about how our deficit spending has come to be entrenched. But there is another factor hiding in the interaction between these two factors, one far more troubling. Although this third factor is not in plain view, once it is seen, it is hard to un-see.

Think back again to what we first learned about American government. One of the most commonly cited causes of the Revolutionary War was that the British Parliament ruled over the American Colonies, but the Colonists could not take part in Parliament. Memorably, Parliament levied taxes upon the Colonists even though the Colonists were given no say in the matter. Taxation without representation, it was called: A distant government was imposing burdens upon some of its citizens who had no way to hold that government accountable for its actions.

In the second paragraph of the Declaration of Independence, Thomas Jefferson carefully set forth the fundamental principle at stake:

> *"We hold these truths to be self-evident: that all men are created equal; that they are endowed by their creator with certain unalienable Rights; that among these are Life, Liberty, and the pursuit of Happiness; that to secure these rights, Governments are instituted among Men, deriving their just powers from the consent of the governed. . . ."*

To Jefferson, it was a self-evident truth that governments derive their *just powers*—meaning *those of their powers that are justified*—from the consent of the governed. Under this principle of democratic legitimacy, powers exercised by a government without the consent of the governed, like taxation without representation, are unjust.

It is in light of this principle that the factors underlying our problem become troubling—even disturbing.

Let's imagine for a moment a hypothetical scenario in which some government passes a law creating a program to spend money for a particular purpose. This spending program is created piece-meal, meaning that it is established because, in isolation, it seems like a good thing to spend money on. Because our hypothetical government is under no pressure to do otherwise, it gives only minimal consideration to how this one spending program will impact its overall finances.

Furthermore, let's imagine that this spending program commits our hypothetical government to spend money in the future. The law has therefore created a mandatory spending program.

Let's then jump ahead a generation—or two, or three—to a time when our hypothetical government has similarly established, piece-meal, a full range of other mandatory spending programs.

Each of those other mandatory spending programs has also committed our hypothetical government to future spending.

However, because its policy-making has been piece-meal, our hypothetical government began to spend in deficit long ago. Once its deficits began, due to the inherent difficulties involved in balancing any budget, any reforms that may reduce the funding of the mandatory spending programs have become practically impossible.

In our hypothetical scenario, the current generation of the governed has found itself with a massive accumulated debt. That current generation does not want deficit spending to continue. However, try as it might, it cannot find a way out of the spending to which it has been committed in laws passed by previous generations.

The current generation of the governed had no say in the spending programs established by previous generations, and those previous generations did not need to bear the cumulative burden of the policies they were establishing. None of that matters: The current generation finds itself trapped in a bind that it did not make. It is beholden, against its own will, to the will of previous generations.

Setting aside our hypothetical scenario, let's consider once more the situation that the Colonists found themselves in prior to the Revolution. Back then, the laws governing the Colonies were made by Parliament. Since the Colonists were excluded from Parliament, Colonial law was being made by people far removed from the concerns of the Colonies, people who would not need to live under the laws they were making. The Colonists were beholden to a government sitting an ocean away, a remote power that was unaccountable to them.

With all of this in mind, consider America's debt problem today. None of us wants America to become insolvent. We differ about the best way to prevent fiscal irresponsibility—often deeply and fundamentally—but none of us is in favor of our government risking financial disaster by continually living beyond its means.

Yet that is exactly what is happening. Our government spends in deficit, year after year, over and over again. Those deficits accumulate, with an endless series of further deficits poised to follow in future years. We seem to have no power to stop this growing mountain of debt.

Technically speaking, we have the ability to end our deficit spending. The Constitution still exists, of course, with all of the mechanisms for democratic accountability that it provides. We still elect Representatives, Senators, and Presidents to make laws, and those officials still exercise their powers subject to our consent.

In practice, however, it seems to be virtually impossible for us to politically coordinate to take our country off the path to insolvency. While we technically have the ability to end our deficit spending, that ability seems to be available to us in name only. In other words, although democratic means for solving our problem are *nominally* available to us, they *effectively* do not exist.

The policies responsible for our reckless accumulation of debt were established by previous generations of Americans. But for all that we may wish to avoid those financially reckless policies, they may as well have been established by the British Parliament, and we may as well be the Colonists beholden to their will. Those policies have effectively become shielded from basic, garden-variety democratic accountability.

Previously-sitting governments almost certainly took the interests of future citizens into account in their policy-making. Then again, members of the British Parliament might also have taken the Colonists' best interests into account, out of the goodness of their hearts. However, any justifiable exercise of governmental power requires more than mere altruism. For governmental rule to be justified, fundamental principles of self-government require the consent of the governed.

Our seemingly inescapable deficit spending is thus far worse than a raw deal. To the extent that policies established by previous generations have burdened us with unwanted deficit spending, and to the extent that it has become effectively impossible for us to politically coordinate to avoid those deficits, those policies are like taxation without representation, and are in violation of basic American principles. That violation, though, merely reflects a deeper violation of fundamental principles of self-government: To bind future citizens to deficit spending that is effectively unavoidable is an unjust exercise of power, because doing so bypasses their consent.

In establishing all of our spending-side and revenue-side policies, previously-sitting governments have committed the current generation of Americans to reckless deficit spending that none of us want, but which we effectively cannot politically coordinate to avoid. The sobering final factor underlying our long-term debt problem is this: *The policies causing our deficit spending are not even democratically legitimate, because they effectively violate the consent of the governed.*

OUR PATH of least resistance in establishing our spending-side and revenue-side policies has led us into deficit spending. From there, our path of least resistance has kept us from escaping our deficit spending. Our deficit spending has become entrenched as a result.

America's process for establishing spending-side and revenue-side policies is broken. The problem is not that we are short-sighted or weak-willed, though. Our ruinous financial path has simply been our path of least resistance.

Based on our inability to resolve our long-term debt problem, some observers might conclude that democracy in America is broken, or perhaps that democracy itself is inherently broken. Our fiscal woes are not, however, a symptom of some inherent problem with democracy.

It is true that each of our spending-side and revenue-side policies was voted upon democratically at one point in time. Those policies, though, were enacted by previously-sitting governments not accountable to us, and the deficits they are causing have become effectively impossible for us to avoid. Our ruinous financial situation has therefore effectively come about without the consent of the governed, and in violation of fundamental principles of self-government. Given this, perhaps it should be expected that something about our democracy may seem to be broken.

Our course toward insolvency is not due to any problem with democracy. We are in an airplane on autopilot, and we are headed for a mountain-side, but not because *we are exercising democracy*. If anything, we are on a course toward insolvency because *democracy is being thwarted.*

• 3 •

WHAT CAN WE DO?

AMERICA'S long-term debt problem is due to our broken process for establishing spending-side and revenue-side policies. In order to solve our problem we must fix that broken process.

To do that, we must resolve the three factors underlying our problem. We must make getting into deficit spending harder than staying out. We must make staying in deficit spending harder than getting out. We must ensure that all of our spending-side and revenue-side policies together do not impose effectively unavoidable burdens and thereby bypass the consent of the governed.

This is a tall order. A solution to our problem, however, cannot rest there. Beyond resolving the underlying factors, there also are a number of characteristics that we should expect a solution to our problem to have.

3.1 A Solution Should Not Seek To Cast Blame

AS A PRELIMINARY MATTER, we must understand that there is no person, organization, or political philosophy that may properly be blamed for our mess. We can't hope to fix our problem by identifying some corrupt element in our midst, a demon that may be cast out once found. There is no single guilty party.

Some would blame our situation on our politicians. This impulse is understandable. Our politicians write the rules under which we live. If things are going wrong, then those rules must surely be involved somehow, and by implication the politicians behind them. Also, politicians are routinely thought of as having a certain slipperiness of character with respect to things like truth and principles, and it can be comforting to hold such people to blame.

Some blame may certainly be placed upon politicians. Not much blame, though. Our politicians do not hold their offices for inexplicable, mystical reasons. They hold their offices because we have elected them.

In our system of government, we are presumed to vote according to our interests, and the people we vote for are presumed to represent those interests. At least in some sense, the politicians we elect are therefore no worse than we deserve. While some blame may be placed upon politicians, some blame must also be placed upon us.

We might complain about the quality of the people running for office. Maybe we only have bad politicians because good people won't run. There are at least two problems with this sort of thinking, though.

One problem is that the type of politician we have is probably the type of politician we should expect to continue having. If political offices have historically been held by people who are less than ideal, we should expect those offices to continue to be held by people who are less than ideal. We can't count on some theoretical regiment of good and wise statesmen to gallop into office and save the day. As the saying goes, we must deal with the world as it is, not as we wish it would be.

Another problem is that there are reasons we have the sort of politicians we have. For example, politicians are the sort of people who are willing to endure a campaign for election, even though their opponents may well pay hundreds of thousands of advertising dollars to reduce them to a simplistic caricature that inspires fear. Most people would not wish to go through what candidates for office are made to go through. Unless the inherent unpleasantries of campaigning for office end, we can't expect changes in the sorts of people who are willing to put themselves forward for office.

Some who are motivated by ideology or partisanship would lay the blame on the party at the other end of the political spectrum. This is doubly misguided.

For one thing, our financial imbalances have come about through piece-meal approval of policies favored by both sides of the spectrum. To blame one side for our deficits and our debt would be to overlook the contributions of the other side. Efforts to place the blame only on one side do more to indicate the policy preferences of the blame-layer than to indicate what is actually at fault.

Beyond that, even supposing that blame could validly be placed solely upon one party, how could that help lead us to a solution? Neither side's entire policy vision is politically achievable. Our country is too solidly divided for the entire set of policies favored by either side to be enacted, let alone endure. Whether as a matter of plain fact, or as a matter of simple practicality, there is no group, no faction, no party that can be held to blame.

In the end, our problem is not *bad people*. Our problem is *a broken process*. If we don't fix that process, we can't solve our problem.

It would be unhelpful at best and counterproductive at worst to concentrate on finding parties to bear blame. Scape-goating will not solve our problem. We have stumbled down this path together, and if we are going to find our way back, we are going to have to find it together, too. A solution to our problem, therefore, should not be fixated on casting blame.

3.2 A Solution Must Be A Constitutional Amendment

WE MUST ALSO UNDERSTAND that our broken process cannot be fixed by *statute* (that is, by laws established through the ordinary lawmaking process). This is for the simple reason that laws passed at one point in time can be overridden by laws passed at a later point in time.

Any solution we may try to implement by statute could also be undone by statute. Any statutory solution to our problem would therefore be a temporary solution at best. Since our problem is a long-term problem, a temporary solution would be no solution at all.

If we are to fix our problem permanently, we must look for a solution that cannot be undone by ordinary statutes. The only way to do that is by amending the Constitution itself.

We have thought about solving our problem by constitutional amendment before. Various balanced budget amendments have been proposed to require that our government not spend more money than it takes in.

A solution to our problem would certainly aim to balance our revenues and spending. Generally speaking, though, we cannot count on a balanced budget amendment to solve our problem.

There are two basic reasons for this. The first reason is that although balanced budget amendments have been under discussion for a long time, they haven't gotten very far. There seems to be something about balanced budget amendments that has kept us from adopting them. This suggests that any constitutional amendment capable of solving our problem will have to be something capable of overcoming whatever has derailed the amendments we have previously considered.

The second reason is that, like a doctor treating the symptom instead of the disease, balanced budget amendments don't address the factors underlying our long-term debt problem. After all, it isn't as if we haven't been trying to balance our budgets. We have spent enormous amounts of effort and political capital over the years in attempting to balance our budgets. It is because balancing our budgets has proven to be so difficult that we have a problem that needs solving in the first place.

We get into deficit spending because it is easier to consider our policies piece-meal than it is to consider our finances as a whole. We stay in deficit spending because it is easier to continue our deficits than it is to balance our budgets. Despite our clear desire to end deficit spending, it has proven to be effectively impossible for us to politically coordinate our way out of these burdens that have been imposed on us by previously-sitting governments, and as a result these deficits are in violation of the consent of the governed.

Instead of addressing these factors, balanced budget amendments merely elevate our existing and long-standing intent to balance our spending and revenues into a demand. Like an ignorant tourist, they amount to *talking louder* instead of *speaking the language*.

The balanced budget amendments that have gotten farthest even seem to anticipate that the balanced budgets they demand may prove to be impossible to enact. These amendments include escape-hatch provisions under which their balanced-budget requirements can be waived upon a vote of three-fifths of both the House of Representatives and the Senate.

With respect to the staying-in factor, the balanced budget amendments would admittedly make it harder to pass budgets that are not balanced. However, because of the escape-hatch provisions, the amendments would still not ensure that passing balanced budgets would be easier than continuing to avoid the inherently difficult budget-balancing process. In any given year, then, staying in deficit spending may still prove to be our path of least resistance.

It may be that the only change in our budgeting process would be an increase in the amount of pressure and heat that would be placed on the citizenry to get it to accept that year's deficit. Each year, the sound and fury of the nation's budgetary politics would be amplified, but we may very well be left with our deficit spending unresolved. The pressure and heat would leave us about as happy with each other as hornets in a shaken-up Mason jar. Then, the next year, we would do it again; then over, and over, and over again.

With respect to the remaining underlying factors, though, the balanced budget amendments do nothing at all. They would not make it easier for us to stay out of deficit spending than to get in, and they would not address the violation of the consent of the governed that our deficits represent. So, assuming that they actually do lead to balanced budgets in any one year, we may still drive our budgets out of balance the next year through further piecemeal spending. The currently-sitting government may still place cumulative spending commitments on future generations that would be effectively impossible to politically coordinate to avoid.

It is conceivable that if we passed a balanced budget amendment, in the course of repeated efforts to comply with it, Congress might eventually pass laws augmenting the amendment that would end up comprehensively addressing the factors underlying our problem. If we were to pass a balanced budget amendment, it is possible that we might end up solving our problem. If we're going to go through all of the effort required to amend the Constitution in order to fix our problem, though, it would make more sense to deal with the factors underlying our problem directly, instead of just hoping that they might someday be dealt with.

More importantly, even if we wind up addressing those factors after enacting a balanced budget amendment, any laws passed to supplement the amendment would not be beyond the reach of ordinary statutes. Whatever additional laws Congress may pass to comprehensively solve our problem could simply be overridden by later statutes when they become inconvenient to follow. Although balanced budget amendments may lead to a solution to our problem, that solution would still be temporary at best.

In order to fix our problem permanently, the solution—the entire solution—must be a constitutional amendment.

3.3 A Solution Must Be Unobjectionable

AMENDING THE CONSTITUTION is very hard. Under Article V of the Constitution, an amendment must first be *proposed* either by two thirds of both the House of Representatives and the Senate, or by a Convention called for by two thirds of the states. After that, a proposed amendment must be *ratified* either by the Legislatures in three fourths of the States, or by Conventions in three fourths of the States.

The country must overwhelmingly support an amendment both in order for it to be proposed and in order for it to be ratified. But how many policies do Americans agree on overwhelmingly? Given our political history, the requirement for that degree of support is an extremely high bar.

In order to achieve the level of support required to propose and ratify any amendment, there would have to be essentially no reason to object to it. That would be hard enough for any proposed policy. Since our problem involves the entire range of our spending-side and revenue-side policies, a solution that nobody could object to seems almost unimaginable.

Nevertheless, because we can only solve our problem by constitutional amendment, any solution—despite being something which would fundamentally and permanently alter the way our government operates—must be essentially unobjectionable.

3.4 A Solution Should Be Procedural

A SOLUTION could be made unobjectionable if it were the sort of thing that no reasonable person could argue with. Unfortunately, although Americans of all political persuasions are rational people, it seems to be in the nature of our partisan politics for us to form opposite opinions about almost every topic. In order to be something that no reasonable person could object to, a proposed solution would have to be absolutely non-partisan. It would have to literally be common sense.

This means that a solution can't enforce any specific policy preferences in the course of balancing the budget. It can't mandate that we preserve health care at the expense of other things, for example, or that we preserve national defense at the expense of other things.

Enforcing any specific policy preference will wind up goring somebody's ox. One end of the political spectrum will be provoked into opposing the solution, and the other end will in turn be provoked—by partisan impulses if nothing else—into opposing that opposition. No matter whose ox is gored, the resulting political polarization will guarantee that the solution will go nowhere.

This may have been part of the reason that recent balanced budget amendments have not gotten very far. Those that have gotten farthest include escape-hatch provisions to waive balanced budget requirements in times of war by a simple majority vote.

Most people would probably see these provisions as a generally wise idea. The country must be defended, after all. However, those provisions invite questions about why other policies or programs, which may be preferred by various people, would not also deserve to be protected in that way.

Interestingly, many provisions of the Constitution do not prescribe specific policy outcomes. Rather, they establish neutral procedures under which our government must operate to arrive at and implement various policies. Such procedures include the process of electing representatives, senators, and presidents, as well as the process of forming and enacting laws. Specific policies are then left to arise out of the day-to-day operation of our political system.

Focusing on mere procedure allows these provisions of the Constitution to be essentially non-controversial. This suggests that a solution to our problem could avoid political polarization by avoiding any and all substantive judgments about how to balance the budget and by instead being entirely procedural in nature. To be as unobjectionable as possible, a solution to our problem should imitate the non-controversial provisions of the Constitution and focus on procedure, too.

3.5 A Solution Should Be Modest

A SOLUTION could also be made unobjectionable if it were minimal or incremental. As a general rule, small changes are the easiest changes to accept. Between two policy changes, if all else is equal, the one that changes things the least will be more politically feasible. To have the best chance of being enacted, a proposed solution would benefit by having as little impact as possible.

Given the nature of our problem, a solution must fundamentally impact both our revenue-side and spending-side policies as well as the process we follow in establishing them. In spite of the fact that it must have far-reaching consequences, in order to be as unobjectionable as possible, a solution to our problem should strive to be modest.

3.6 A Solution Must Be Complete

FINALLY, A SOLUTION should not depend upon any altruistic action on our part in the future, and should in and of itself do everything that must be done to solve our problem.

It is said that the price of liberty is eternal vigilance. That saying captures an admirable attitude toward citizenship. It's a nice saying.

In practice, though, eternal vigilance is too exhausting. Being people, we are flawed, as are our elected officials. To make the success of a solution depend upon continuous victory in an eternal battle would be to ensure the solution's eventual failure.

We cannot rely upon eternal vigilance. Instead, once a solution has been set in place it must be sufficient to lead us to balanced budgets and keep us there with little to no additional lawmaking required. The solution must make balanced budgets no more than the natural result of our political process in action. To end our problem once and for all, a solution to our problem must be complete.

SO, A SOLUTION to our long-term debt problem cannot seek to lay blame and will have to be a constitutional amendment. Because of the level of support required to enact constitutional amendments, a solution will have to be essentially unobjectionable, meaning that it must be entirely reasonable and must avoid provoking partisan resistance.

A proposed solution could be made unobjectionable by being procedural in nature. It could also be made unobjectionable—despite having far-reaching consequences—by being modest in scope. As if that weren't enough, a solution must be complete, perpetually fulfilling its purpose on its own once enacted.

A proposed solution must be capable of resolving our problem, which has so far proven to be massive and intractable. Yet it must somehow be inoffensive enough to actually be enacted.

In other words, a solution to our problem must seemingly do nothing, while actually doing everything.

• 4 •

A GLIMMER

GIVEN THE CHARACTERISTICS that we should expect a solution to our long-term debt problem to have, any search for such a solution would surely seem doomed to failure from the start. There may be, however, a glimmer of hope.

Consider our system of separation of powers and checks-and-balances in government. We have long recognized that citizens may be protected from improper exercises of government power by splitting governmental authority into separate and co-equal branches and establishing a system of checks and balances between them. If one branch tries to improperly expand its power, the other branches will act to limit that expansion, motivated by a jealous impulse to guard their own power. Such an arrangement can harness the otherwise destructive power-seeking impulse of government and put it to good use.

Consider also the basic structure of a market economy. We have long recognized that the greater good may be enhanced by economic transactions even though each party to the transactions may only be acting selfishly. An economic actor serving selfish ends (such as attempting to increase the actor's own assets) must bind those ends to the ends of others to gain the benefits of economic transactions. This leads to the "invisible hand" observed by Adam Smith: that an individual, by pursuing his own interest, "frequently promotes that of the society more effectually than when he really intends to promote it." A market arrangement can thus harness the selfish impulses of individuals, which might otherwise be destructive, and use them for the benefit of others.

Our experience with such arrangements suggests that powerful destructive forces can be brought to heel and even turned to our advantage. If there were some way to harness the destructive forces behind our problem, perhaps they could be made to serve the common good, too.

• 5 •

A SOLUTION

WHAT FOLLOWS is a solution to our long-term debt problem. It resolves the factors underlying our problem, and it does so in a way that is mindful of the characteristics that we should expect a solution to have.

It is a constitutional amendment, but it doesn't just demand balanced budgets as a balanced budget amendment would. Instead, it creates conditions under which we will be naturally guided to our budgets ourselves. It is, for lack of a better term, a Solvency Amendment.

This Solvency Amendment is like a machine with interlocking parts, each part serving a particular function. For such machines, once the functions of each part are understood, and upon understanding the way the parts interact with each other, the operation of the machine as a whole becomes clear. A car, for example, has an engine, a transmission, axles, and wheels, each of which serves its own function. It is the interaction between these interlocking parts—the engine extracting energy from fuel, the transmission using that energy to rotate the axles, and the rotation of the axles in turn spinning the wheels—that makes the car move.

The Solvency Amendment has five interlocking parts. Each part is introduced below, one at a time, along with a discussion about its functions and the way in which it interacts with the other parts. Each part is then presented in the language of a constitutional amendment. Once all five parts are understood, the operation of the Amendment as a whole will become clear.

These interlocking parts make the Amendment at least somewhat complex. If our problem could be solved by something trivial, though, we would have solved it a long time ago. Our problem has proven to be quite resilient. Some complexity in solving it may just come with the territory.

Many of our existing constitutional amendments are divided into Sections, each of which includes one or more Clauses (i.e., sentences). In a similar manner, the Solvency Amendment has five Sections. The first four parts of the Amendment are set forth among various Clauses in Sections 1 through 4, while Section 5 alone sets forth the fifth and final part.

5.1 A Budgeting Sequence

THE FIRST PART of the Solvency Amendment is a budgeting process with four sequential steps. This sequence is outside of and in addition to existing federal budgeting processes.

Under this four-step budgeting sequence, four amounts associated with the budget are established every year, one at a time. The amounts established in the budgeting sequence will then be applied to our government's spending beginning in the next calendar year. This gives our government a year to establish those amounts before they will come into force.

The Amendment requires this budgeting sequence to start after Congress begins its first meeting of the year. Regarding that first meeting, Section 2 of the 20th Amendment states:

Amendment 20, Section 2.
The Congress shall assemble at least once in every year, and such meeting shall begin at noon on the 3d day of January, unless they shall by law appoint a different day.

Under the 20th Amendment, the Legislature must meet each year, either on January 3rd or on some other day that Congress appoints. Given this, the four-step budgeting sequence begins every year at noon on January 3rd (or on whatever other day Congress may appoint).

In the first step of the sequence, the Amendment requires that our government establish a number corresponding with an overall *outlay limit.* In the next step, our government must establish a first allowance of the outlay limit to cover spending in the next year that cannot be avoided by passing new laws, like interest payments on the public debts—i.e., an *interest allowance.* In the next step, our government must establish a second allowance of the outlay limit to cover spending that it has not yet committed itself to, but will commit itself to in the next year—i.e., a *discretionary allowance.* In the last step, our government must establish a third allowance of the outlay limit to cover spending that it has already committed itself to in past years, but which is possible for it to avoid by passing a new law—i.e., a *mandatory allowance.*

The first budgetary amount—the outlay limit—is basically what it sounds like: a number to which our government's total spending in the next year will be limited. At a fundamental level, any effort to balance a budget must include such a number. If spending is to be limited, there must be some number to which it will be limited.

However, the outlay limit can't simply be whatever number our government wishes. After all, if our problem is that we are chronically not living within our means, then the outlay limit must have some relationship with our means or it cannot help us live within them.

The third part of the Amendment will address the particulars of setting the outlay limit and how it will relate to our means. For now, think of the outlay limit as some number that will reasonably reflect our means for the following year.

The second budgetary amount—the interest allowance—is for purposes of spending in the next year that cannot be avoided by passing new laws. Some of the spending that our government is committed to cannot be evaded legislatively, meaning that getting out of it isn't just a matter of passing a law removing the obligation to spend that money. It is simply not possible to politically coordinate to avoid such commitments.

Such spending would include contractual obligations, for example, which cannot be arbitrarily cancelled by new laws. In particular, such spending would also include costs due to servicing the public debts, i.e., interest payments. The United States cannot enter into public debts and just nullify them later at its whim in order to avoid the costs of servicing them.

In contrast, the third and fourth budgetary amounts—the discretionary allowance and the mandatory allowance—are for purposes of spending that *can* be avoided by passing new laws.

For example, the discretionary allowance is for purposes of spending that our government might commit itself to in the next year, but to which it has not yet committed itself. It is possible for our government to politically coordinate to avoid such spending—indeed, such spending commitments have not yet even been made.

Similarly, the mandatory allowance is for purposes of spending that our government has already committed itself to, but which is avoidable by passing new laws. Unlike spending under the interest allowance, even though our government has already committed itself to such spending in past years, it is possible to avoid mandatory spending given sufficient political coordination.

For both discretionary and mandatory spending, it may well have proven to be effectively impossible to politically coordinate in order to avoid spending commitments. For the purposes of the Amendment, the most important aspect of such spending is that it is *possible* for our government to politically coordinate to avoid it, no matter how difficult it may be to do so in practice.

The budgeting sequence serves two functions. The first function is to establish separate budgetary amounts for the other parts of the Amendment to use. Each of the three types of spending corresponding with the three allowances is different in character. For example, spending due to debt servicing and mandatory spending are types of spending that our government is in various ways committed to, while such commitments have not yet been made for discretionary spending. On the other hand, unlike spending due to debt servicing, both discretionary spending and mandatory spending are possible for us to avoid.

Because of these differences in character, each of the three types of spending relates differently to the factors underlying our problem. Any solution to our problem would therefore have to treat them differently. By establishing the various budgetary amounts, the budgeting sequence provides handles for the other parts of the Amendment to use in resolving the factors underlying our problem.

The second function the budgeting sequence serves is to make it easier to balance the budget. By separating out different types of spending into the various budgetary amounts, the massive, complicated problem that we have so far been incapable of resolving is reduced to smaller, more easily resolvable problems.

By requiring that these budgetary amounts be established in separate steps, with each step to be completed before the next begins, the budgeting sequence also reduces difficulties of political coordination that might otherwise exist if all the various portions of the budget were to be established at the same time. If debate and discussion for one budgetary amount must be complete before debate and discussion for the next budgetary amount may begin, it may be easier to determine an appropriate value for each budgetary amount due to its relative isolation from debate regarding the others.

The following language presents the budgeting sequence as part of the text of a constitutional amendment. Before considering that text, it may be helpful to keep in mind a couple of things about the language used in the Amendment.

First of all, note that the Amendment uses the phrase "by law" regarding various congressional actions, such as the establishment of the four budgetary amounts in the budgeting sequence. The phrase "by law" refers to the ordinary legislative process that Congress follows when making laws, which is described in Section 7 of Article I of the Constitution. Under that process, both the House of Representatives and the Senate pass a Bill, which then goes to the President. If the President signs the Bill, it becomes a Law. Alternatively, if the President vetoes the Bill, the Bill may still become a Law if both the House and the Senate pass it by a two-thirds vote.

By providing that Congress take a particular action "by law," the Constitution requires that the action be taken through the process just described. As a result, language in the Solvency Amendment directing Congress to "by law establish" something means that the Legislative and Executive branches must debate that thing through the standard and familiar law-making process.

Secondly, note that the Amendment uses the term "shall." This is important, because the terms "shall" and "may" have legal significance. Legally, when an entity "shall" do something, then it must do that thing. It has no choice. On the other hand, when an entity "may" do something, then the entity can either do that thing, or not do that thing, depending upon what it chooses.

Therefore, the phrase "Congress may by law establish" means that our government would have discretion in making a particular law. On the other hand, the phrase "Congress shall by law establish" leaves no wiggle-room: our government must make the particular law described, without exception.

The Budgeting Sequence

Section 1. The outlay limit

Every year, after the beginning of its first assembly, Congress shall by law establish an outlay limit for the next year.

Section 2. The first allowance [the interest allowance]

After establishing the outlay limit, Congress shall by law establish a first allowance of the outlay limit, which shall be for the purposes of Expenditures in the next year that are not avoidable by law, to include the costs of servicing the public Debts.

Section 3. The second allowance [the discretionary allowance]

After establishing the first allowance, Congress shall by law establish a second allowance of the outlay limit, which shall be for the purposes of any amounts that Congress may reserve for Expenditures in the next year under Appropriations to be made in the next year.

Section 4. The third allowance [the mandatory allowance]

After establishing the second allowance, Congress shall by law establish a third allowance of the outlay limit, which shall be for the purposes of Expenditures in the next year under Appropriations made before the next year that are avoidable by law.

The budgeting sequence does not resolve our long-term debt problem by itself. Although it establishes various different budgetary amounts, these amounts aren't yet being used to bring our government's budgets into balance.

5.2 Spending Conditions

THE SECOND PART of the Solvency Amendment begins to use the budgetary amounts determined by the budgeting sequence. It does so by making our government's spending subject to certain conditions: the establishment and the value of each budgetary amount.

In order to understand the second part of the Solvency Amendment, consider the following Clauses of Article I, Section 8 of the Constitution, which deal with our government's Receipts and Expenditures:

> ***Article I, Section 8.*** [Clauses 1 & 2]
> *The Congress shall have Power[:]*
> *To lay and collect Taxes, Duties, Imposts and Excises, to pay the Debts and provide for the common Defence and general Welfare of the United States; but all Duties, Imposts and Excises shall be uniform throughout the United States;*
> *To borrow money on the credit of the United States;*
> . . . .
>
> ***Article I, Section 9.*** [Clause 7]
> . . . .
> *No Money shall be drawn from the Treasury, but in Consequence of Appropriations made by Law; and a regular Statement and Account of the Receipts and Expenditures of all public Money shall be published from time to time.*
> . . . .

These Clauses describe the process the United States government must follow in acquiring and spending money.

With respect to Receipts (that is, revenue or income), Congress may use various mechanisms to raise money (i.e., laying and collecting "Taxes, Duties, Imposts, and Excises"). Congress may also "borrow money on the credit of the United States," meaning that it may assume debts that it promises to repay later in return for receiving money that may be spent now. Those Receipts will then be available in the Treasury.

With respect to Expenditures (that is, spending or outlays), Money may only be drawn from the Treasury "in Consequence of Appropriations made by law." In order to spend money, our government must first pass a law (under the standard law-making process) to *appropriate* that money from the Treasury. The corresponding money may then be *drawn* from the Treasury, to be spent as appropriated.

For the purposes of the Solvency Amendment, the significance of these portions of the Constitution is that the appropriation of money and the drawing of money are two distinct steps in the process that the United States government must go through to spend money. In particular, appropriations are the specific way in which mandatory spending programs commit our government to spend money in future years. When our government has committed itself to mandatory spending, it has established appropriations that will permit the drawing of money in future years.

The function of the second part of the Amendment is to introduce two types of intermediate conditions into this process of spending money, and to permit the drawing of money in the following year only in accordance with those spending conditions. One type of condition restricts the timing of the drawing of money. The other type of condition restricts the total amount of money that can be drawn.

Because of the spending conditions, under the Amendment, an existing appropriation of money will no longer be sufficient to permit the corresponding money to be drawn from the Treasury in the following year. Instead, before that money may be drawn, the conditions on timing and total amounts must also be satisfied.

With respect to the timing of the drawing of money, the spending conditions prevent money from being drawn for purposes under each allowance until the corresponding allowance has been established. Under these conditions, money for purposes falling under a particular allowance may only be drawn in the next year once that particular allowance has been established by law (in accordance with the budgeting sequence).

For example, money for purposes falling under the discretionary allowance may only be drawn from the Treasury in the next year after the discretionary allowance has been established. Similarly, money for purposes falling under the mandatory allowance may only be drawn from the Treasury in the next year after the mandatory allowance has been established.

So, unless the budgeting sequence has been completed within the year and the budgetary amounts have been established, there will be one or more purposes for which money cannot be drawn from the Treasury in the following year, even if that money has already been appropriated (as is the case with mandatory spending). This will provide an irresistible motivation for Congress to satisfy the requirements of the budgeting sequence before the year is over and the budgetary amounts come into force.

More significantly, with respect to the total amount of money drawn, the spending conditions prevent money from being drawn for purposes under each allowance beyond the value established for each allowance. Instead, money may only be drawn for purposes under each allowance up to the limit of each allowance.

Due to the spending conditions, appropriations made by our government in past years—which are especially problematic with respect to the consent of the governed—will no longer be sufficient in and of themselves to result in the actual drawing of the corresponding money. Even if our government has in past years established appropriations of money intended to be binding in the next year, that money may only be drawn up to the limit of the mandatory allowance.

The Spending Conditions

Section 1. The outlay limit

Money shall not be drawn from the Treasury in the next year except in accordance with this Amendment and under this Constitution.

Every year, after the beginning of its first assembly, Congress shall by law establish an outlay limit for the next year.

Section 2. The first allowance [the interest allowance]

After establishing the outlay limit, Congress shall by law establish a first allowance of the outlay limit, which shall be for the purposes of Expenditures in the next year that are not avoidable by law, to include the costs of servicing the public Debts.

Upon establishing the first allowance, Money may be drawn from the Treasury in the next year for purposes under the first allowance, up to the limit of the first allowance.

Section 3. The second allowance [the discretionary allowance]

After establishing the first allowance, Congress shall by law establish a second allowance of the outlay limit, which shall be for the purposes of any amounts that Congress may reserve for Expenditures in the next year under Appropriations to be made in the next year.

Upon establishing the second allowance, Money may also be drawn from the Treasury in the next year for purposes under the second allowance, up to the limit of the second allowance.

Section 4. The third allowance [the mandatory allowance]

After establishing the second allowance, Congress shall by law establish a third allowance of the outlay limit, which shall be for the purposes of Expenditures in the next year under Appropriations made before the next year that are avoidable by law.

Upon establishing the third allowance, Money may also be drawn from the Treasury in the next year for purposes under the third allowance, up to the limit of the third allowance.

The budgeting sequence and the spending conditions still do not resolve our long-term debt problem, though. Although they limit spending for purposes under each of the three allowances up to the limit of the corresponding allowance, those budgetary amounts are not yet constrained themselves. Indeed, the three allowances are not yet even related to the outlay limit. If the allowances are merely set to whatever numbers our government picks, they will likely be set to whatever amounts are required to cover our current levels of spending, and will be useless in helping us live within our means.

5.3 Budget Constraints

THE BUDGETING SEQUENCE DESCRIBED ABOVE establishes the outlay limit and the three allowances, and the spending conditions described above limit the drawing of money under each allowance to the amount of each allowance. Building upon this groundwork, the third part of the Solvency Amendment establishes constraints upon the budgetary amounts themselves.

These budget constraints limit the values of the various budgetary amounts, beginning with the outlay limit. As discussed above regarding the budgeting sequence, for the outlay limit to be useful in balancing our budget, it must be a reasonable estimate of our means for the following year. However, our government can't forecast its income for the next year with absolute certainty. Arriving at an estimate that will be a reasonable reflection of our means for the following year is inherently tricky.

The most basic estimate of our government's income would be our government's receipts in the previous year. However, while the general historical trend is that governmental receipts have grown over time, the rate of that growth hasn't been constant and smooth. Receipts have instead fluctuated from year to year, and have even decreased in difficult economic times. The possibility that the outlay limit could shrink from one year to the next might be enough in and of itself to make the Amendment politically unacceptable.

If the outlay limit were instead constrained to an average of our government's receipts over a number of past years, the rate of growth of the outlay limit could be made more constant and smooth, and the impact of decreasing receipts in bad economic times could be moderated. However, in particularly bad economic times, even an average of receipts might decrease.

The likelihood of a decrease in an average of receipts could be reduced by increasing the number of years over which the average is taken. As more years are included in such an average, though, the average would reach further back into the past. In good economic times—meaning, in times following the general trend of increasing revenues—the average may include years in which governmental receipts were much, much lower. This would in turn drag the average down.

The risk of dragging down the average in good years could be reduced by adjusting the receipts of earlier years to account for such things as inflation, or population growth. That would invite questions about the proper determination of inflation and population growth, making an already complicated process even more complicated.

For simplicity's sake, the Amendment constrains the outlay limit to not exceed the maximum revenue of any past year. The outlay limit would thereby follow the general trend over time toward increasing governmental receipts, while eliminating the potential for year-to-year reductions in the outlay limit in difficult economic times that might otherwise make the Amendment politically unacceptable.

Additionally, by relating the outlay limit to previous receipts in a straightforward way, little to no debate will be required to establish the outlay limit. Establishing the outlay limit would become a *ministerial* act, meaning that it would require only the simple determination of objective facts. Political wrangling to establish the outlay limit would thereby be minimized, if not eliminated.

The budget constraints also make the establishment of the interest allowance a ministerial act. Under the Amendment, the interest allowance is constrained to be sufficient to cover the purposes under it. Our government would only need to figure out its unavoidable obligations in the next year, such as its obligations due to servicing the public debts. Determining this amount should be a matter of relatively straightforward data collection and calculation. Therefore, as with the outlay limit, political debate in establishing the interest allowance could be minimized.

With respect to the discretionary allowance and the mandatory allowance, the budget constraints give the Amendment its backbone. Specifically, the Amendment constrains the sum of the discretionary and mandatory allowances to not exceed whatever is left of the outlay limit once the interest allowance is removed, an amount that the Amendment calls *the remainder*. Notably, because both the establishment of the outlay limit and the establishment of the interest allowance are ministerial acts, the establishment of the remainder would effectively be a ministerial act as well.

Recall that the budgeting sequence requires that the interest allowance be established before the discretionary allowance, and requires that the discretionary allowance be established before the mandatory allowance. The establishment of the allowances in this order has implications in the context of the budget constraints.

Specifically, once the interest allowance is established, it is subtracted from the outlay limit to establish the remainder. After that, once the discretionary allowance is established, it is subtracted from the remainder, and the mandatory allowance is constrained to whatever is left over.

The establishment of the discretionary allowance therefore effectively becomes a decision about how to divide the remainder between discretionary spending and mandatory spending. This is the single non-ministerial act involved in establishing the budgetary amounts. The establishment of the discretionary allowance will instead need to be resolved through political debate.

As mentioned above, the three types of spending under the three allowances relate differently to the factors underlying our problem. One function of the budget constraints is to treat each of the three allowances differently, in accordance with the different natures of each of the three types of spending, in order to resolve the factors underlying our problem.

With respect to the interest allowance, our problem has to do with spending that is possible for us to avoid, but which we are effectively unable to politically coordinate to avoid. Spending that falls under the interest allowance is therefore unrelated to our problem. Since it is unavoidable to begin with, attempting to avoid it would be pointless.

Furthermore, the interest allowance represents spending that in some sense should be considered more obligatory than other types of spending. We have to spend money to service public debts. (Indeed, the sort of spending that would fall under the interest allowance has a better claim to being considered "mandatory" than what we have come to refer to as "mandatory spending.") It is therefore fitting and proper to constrain the interest allowance to be sufficient to cover the purposes under it.

With respect to the discretionary and mandatory allowances, any effort to balance the budget would inherently have to impact discretionary spending, mandatory spending, or both. Any such effort would also inherently wind up splitting the budget between discretionary spending and mandatory spending. The constraints upon the discretionary and mandatory allowances therefore do no more than what any attempt to balance the budget would have to do.

The effective constraint on the mandatory allowance is proper for another reason, too. Although both discretionary spending programs and mandatory spending programs tend to acquire political inertia, mandatory spending is particularly problematic. Since mandatory spending has been established by previously-sitting governments, the consent of the governed is violated when such spending becomes effectively unavoidable. However, by limiting the discretionary and mandatory allowances to the remainder, spending under the mandatory allowance becomes subject to the consent of the currently-sitting government.

Due to the spending conditions, spending under the mandatory allowance may proceed up to but no further than the limit of the mandatory allowance. This means that it doesn't matter how much money has been appropriated for such purposes in past years: mandatory spending is made wholly dependent upon a decision of the currently-sitting government. With the budget constraints, the Solvency Amendment thus restores the consent of the governed, resolving one of the factors underlying our long-term debt problem.

The Budget Constraints

Section 1. The outlay limit

Money shall not be drawn from the Treasury in the next year except in accordance with this Amendment and under this Constitution.

Every year, after the beginning of its first assembly, Congress shall by law establish an outlay limit for the next year.

The outlay limit shall not exceed the maximum total Receipts of public Money from Taxes, Duties, Imposts, and Excises in any previous year.

Section 2. The first allowance [the interest allowance]

After establishing the outlay limit, Congress shall by law establish a first allowance of the outlay limit, which shall be for the purposes of Expenditures in the next year that are not avoidable by law, to include the costs of servicing the public Debts.

The first allowance shall be sufficient to satisfy the purposes under the first allowance; and any part of the outlay limit in excess of the first allowance shall be the remainder of the outlay limit.

Upon establishing the first allowance, Money may be drawn from the Treasury in the next year for purposes under the first allowance, up to the limit of the first allowance.

Section 3. The second allowance [the discretionary allowance]

. . . .

Section 4. The third allowance [the mandatory allowance]

After establishing the second allowance, Congress shall by law establish a third allowance of the outlay limit, which shall be for the purposes of Expenditures in the next year under Appropriations made before the next year that are avoidable by law.

The sum of the second allowance and the third allowance shall not exceed any remainder.

Upon establishing the third allowance, Money may also be drawn from the Treasury in the next year for purposes under the third allowance, up to the limit of the third allowance.

The budget constraints resolve one of the underlying factors. However, establishing the discretionary allowance would likely require a fierce and highly contentious political debate every year.

In addition, there will almost certainly be *funding shortfalls*, meaning that the amount of money that the discretionary and mandatory allowances will permit our government to spend will fall short of the amount of money our government may be inclined to spend under those allowances. The budget constraints do not make it easy to resolve such shortfalls. Indeed, if there were nothing more to the Solvency Amendment, it would be making the same sort of bare demand to balance discretionary spending and mandatory spending within their allowances that balanced budget amendments make regarding spending as a whole.

This is because the first three parts by themselves do not resolve the remaining two underlying factors. With respect to getting into deficit spending, they do not make it easier to consider our policies as a whole instead of considering our policies piece-meal. With respect to staying in deficit spending, they do not make it easier to balance our budgets.

In addition to resolving the underlying factors, though, it is just as important that the Amendment have the characteristics we should expect a solution to have for the solution it presents to be politically achievable. The Amendment should strive to have only a modest impact, for example. Yet by splitting the remainder between discretionary spending and mandatory spending, it would seem that the pain of balancing the budget would be spread about as far and wide as possible. Without more, it is hard to see how funding shortfalls can be resolved in a way that would not leave the Amendment politically dead on arrival.

While the final part of the Amendment provides the ultimate resolution to these problems, the fourth part closes much of the gap.

5.4 Balancing Provisions

THE FOURTH PART of the Solvency Amendment addresses the remaining underlying factors. It has been easier for us to get into deficit spending than to stay out because we consider our policies piece-meal instead of as a whole. At the same time, it has been easier for us to stay in deficit spending than to get out because it is just plain hard to balance our budget.

Any solution to our problem would need to help us consider our policies as a whole, and would need to help us balance our budgets. The fourth part implements two balancing provisions to provide that assistance.

The first balancing provision tightens up a loose end left by the budget constraints by helping us establish the discretionary allowance. As mentioned above, under the Amendment, the discretionary and mandatory allowances are collectively limited to the remainder. Since the establishment of the discretionary allowance also effectively establishes the mandatory allowance, the discretionary allowance is likely to be established only after fierce political debate.

When the time comes, the most obvious starting point for that debate would be with discretionary and mandatory allowances that most closely reflect the relative priorities that we currently assign to those types of spending. We could roughly estimate those relative priorities by determining the portion of our current spending that is devoted to discretionary spending and the portion of our current spending that is devoted to mandatory spending. Those portions, when considered in proportion to each other, would reasonably reflect the relative priorities that we currently assign to discretionary and mandatory spending.

After debating the value of the discretionary allowance, we might not end up establishing the discretionary and mandatory allowances in the same proportions that we currently devote to those types of spending. However, those proportions would be a decent educated guess as to where we would be likely to end up.

Due to the budgeting sequence and the spending conditions, no discretionary spending could proceed in the next year until the discretionary allowance has been established. Similarly, no mandatory spending could proceed in the next year until the mandatory allowance has been established, which in turn depends upon the discretionary allowance being established. Nobody in our government would allow all spending of both types to crash to a halt. As a result, no matter how fierce the political debate would be, it would finish before the end of the year.

We would never have to worry about failing to establish the discretionary and mandatory allowances. However, we could end up with an exercise in political brinksmanship—and since the establishment of both the outlay limit and the interest allowance would be ministerial acts, that brinksmanship could last up to a year. That would be an unpleasant amount of political heat to endure every year, especially since our relative priorities are not likely to change all that much from one year to the next.

Because of this, the first balancing provision specifies a default proportion for splitting the remainder between the discretionary allowance and the mandatory allowance. Unless Congress acts to the contrary, the discretionary allowance will be established to be the same fraction of the remainder as it had been in the previous year.

With this default splitting proportion, Congress will only need to step in to establish the discretionary allowance if our relative priorities between discretionary spending and mandatory spending have changed. If our relative priorities have not changed, then establishing both the discretionary and mandatory allowances will become yet another ministerial act. The establishment of the discretionary allowance would therefore no longer risk causing an unpleasant and unnecessary yearly dose of political brinksmanship.

The First
Balancing Provision

Section 3. The second allowance [the discretionary allowance]

After establishing the first allowance, Congress shall by law establish a second allowance of the outlay limit, which shall be for the purposes of any amounts that Congress may reserve for Expenditures in the next year under Appropriations to be made in the next year.

Unless Congress establishes the second allowance otherwise before the beginning of the next year, the second allowance shall be established so that the Proportion which it shall bear to any remainder is equal to the Proportion which the previously-established second allowance shall have born to the previous remainder.

Upon establishing the second allowance, Money may also be drawn from the Treasury in the next year for purposes under the second allowance, up to the limit of the second allowance.

While the budget constraints give the Solvency Amendment a backbone, the second balancing provision gives the Amendment muscle. As mentioned above, under the Amendment, our government will almost certainly be inclined to spend more money on discretionary and mandatory spending programs than the discretionary and mandatory allowances will permit. By themselves, the first three parts of the Amendment would amount to the same sort of bare demand for budget-balancing that is made by balanced budget amendments.

The resolution of such funding shortfalls is the long-frustrated goal of all of the effort we have spent over time trying to balance our budgets. The second balancing provision helps us to resolve those shortfalls and bring our budgets into balance.

The second balancing provision addresses spending under the mandatory allowance. Due to the spending conditions, when there is a shortfall between appropriations established in past years for mandatory spending programs and the mandatory allowance, there will be some portion of the appropriations for which money cannot be drawn from the Treasury. The Amendment will prohibit any spending under the mandatory allowance that is in excess of the allowance itself.

The second balancing provision resolves such shortfalls by overriding those appropriations established in past years and reinstating them to be as large as possible without exceeding the mandatory allowance. To do this, the Amendment requires Congress to determine the total amount of money necessary to fully cover the next year's mandatory spending. If there is a funding shortfall under the mandatory allowance, then the mandatory allowance will be some fraction of that total amount.

The second balancing provision uses that fraction as a default reinstatement proportion for resolving shortfalls under the mandatory allowance. Every appropriation of money for mandatory spending is reinstated up to that fraction of the previously-established appropriation. Any shortfalls in the mandatory allowance will therefore be carried over proportionally, across the board, to every mandatory spending program.

If the Solvency Amendment were to end with the second balancing provision, two things would be true. The first thing is that the Amendment would effectively be making an across-the-board cut to all mandatory spending. The second thing is that the Amendment would never be ratified, even assuming that it could draw enough political support to be proposed at all. The second balancing provision, without more, would politically sink the Amendment.

The political viability of the Solvency Amendment is ultimately secured by Section 5. Before proceeding to Section 5, though, there are two things left to be said about the second balancing provision.

The first thing is that even if political viability was not an issue, carrying over a shortfall in the mandatory allowance to every mandatory spending program in an across-the-board manner would be a pretty rough way to squeeze our mandatory spending into the mandatory spending allowance. Proportional reinstatement may not be the best reflection of the relative priorities that we would assign to each of various mandatory spending programs. That budget-balancing method would seem to leave no room for other budget-balancing methods that might better reflect our relative priorities.

Recognizing this, the Amendment provides that the default reinstatement proportion is just that—a default. Under the second balancing provision, if Congress wishes to, it may deviate from the default reinstatement proportion and may instead establish alternate reinstatement proportions, or even entirely different manners of reinstating appropriations made in past years.

Congress may, for example, select alternate reinstatement proportions to apply to spending under each spending program, so that the reinstatement proportion applied to some spending programs may be greater than the default proportion, and the reinstatement proportion applied to other spending programs may be less than the default proportion. Alternatively, Congress may establish a manner of fitting mandatory spending within the mandatory spending allowance that is not based upon reinstatement proportions at all. Thus, if there is an alternative to the default reinstatement proportion that Congress would prefer, Congress may have it.

However, unless there are some limits to those potential alternatives, Congress would be tempted to violate the mandatory allowance. Congress might, for example, establish alternate reinstatement proportions greater than the default reinstatement proportion for every mandatory spending program. This would end up recreating within the mandatory allowance the problem that makes our overall budget hard to balance: some spending must go, but all spending is protected.

The Amendment therefore stipulates that any alternate reinstatement proportions or other manners of reinstating appropriations will only be valid if they will not violate the mandatory allowance. Furthermore, instead of attempting to determine which part of an alternative budget-balancing method is at fault, the Amendment will hold the entire alternate method to be void. So, the second balancing provision allows Congress to reinstate appropriations under the mandatory allowance either in accordance with the default reinstatement proportion, or in accordance with any alternate budget-balancing method that does not violate the mandatory allowance.

The second thing left to be said about the second balancing provision is that even though it addresses spending under the mandatory allowance, it will impact spending under the discretionary allowance as well. The second balancing provision only provides guidance regarding mandatory spending because mandatory spending—unlike discretionary spending—is based upon something that already exists: appropriations established in past years. It is hard to provide specific guidance with respect to appropriations under the discretionary allowance, since those appropriations do not yet even exist.

However, our budgets are not being broken by mandatory spending alone. They are being broken by both discretionary spending and mandatory spending combined. Any solution to our problem must therefore address both.

The second balancing provision addresses discretionary spending, albeit indirectly. As with mandatory spending, the Amendment will prohibit any spending under the discretionary allowance that is in excess of the discretionary allowance. As with mandatory spending, it will be inherently hard to fit discretionary spending within the discretionary allowance.

While mandatory spending will be directly modified, discretionary spending will take place in the inescapable shadow of the second balancing provision. It will simply not be credible for advocates of discretionary spending to argue that fitting discretionary spending under its allowance is a problem that is too difficult to resolve. The second balancing provision will provide an immediate and permanent example that will be impossible to ignore.

So, when the question arises as to exactly how to modify the various discretionary spending programs in order to fit discretionary spending within its allowance, an answer will be ready at hand: in a manner similar to the way in which the second default proportion fits mandatory spending under its allowance. When actual appropriations do become established under the discretionary allowance, the obvious way to fit them within the discretionary allowance will be through the use of something like the second balancing provision.

The Second
Balancing Provision

Section 4. The third allowance [the mandatory allowance]

After establishing the second allowance, Congress shall by law establish a third allowance of the outlay limit, which shall be for the purposes of Expenditures in the next year under Appropriations made before the next year that are avoidable by law.

The sum of the second allowance and the third allowance shall not exceed any remainder.

Congress shall determine the amount sufficient to satisfy the purposes under the third allowance, and if that amount should exceed the third allowance, any and all Appropriations of Money in the next year for each such purpose shall be reinstated in the Proportion which the third allowance shall bear to that amount.

Congress may by law provide for alternate reinstatement Proportions or other manners of reinstating Appropriations of Money for purposes under the third allowance; but no such provision shall be valid unless the combination of all such provisions does not violate the third allowance.

Upon establishing the third allowance, Money may also be drawn from the Treasury in the next year for purposes under the third allowance, up to the limit of the third allowance.

The default reinstatement proportion is a crude sort of mechanism for resolving funding shortfalls. It has the advantage, however, of mathematical certainty. When considering the basic question of how our spending could be made to fit within a spending constraint, we know that proportional reinstatement would work.

Taken together, the balancing provisions resolve the two remaining factors underlying our long-term debt problem. In the first part of the Amendment, the budgeting sequence splits our spending into various allowances to deal with different types of spending. In the second part, the spending conditions require all of our spending to fit within those allowances. In the third part, the budget constraints limit the allowances themselves. Then, in the fourth part, the balancing provisions help us adjust our spending to fit within the allowances and balance our budgets in the process.

We already know that if we are balancing our budgets, we will need to spend less money than we may otherwise be inclined to spend in order to live within our means. We already know that lowering our spending involves hard decisions. This is the staying-in factor: that staying in deficit spending is easier than getting out, because balancing any budget is just plain hard.

The balancing provisions resolve this factor by simplifying the process of balancing the budget. First, the balancing provisions establish reasonable default conditions for balanced budgets. The default splitting proportion of the first balancing provision reasonably reflects our relative priorities between discretionary spending and mandatory spending. Similarly, the default reinstatement proportion of the second balancing provision reasonably reflects our relative priorities among the various mandatory spending programs.

Then, if these proportions are found to be less reasonable than other potential proportions, the balancing provisions make Congress perfectly free to override them. The balancing provisions do not impose requirements, but merely provide guidance. They are defaults, not destiny.

Indeed, with the default splitting proportion and the default reinstatement proportion, Congress will not need to make any decisions at all to establish the mandatory allowance and balance spending to which we are already committed. Furthermore, the example provided by the second balancing provision will guide Congress to similarly balance spending that is yet to be established under the discretionary allowance. We will never again need to rely upon the goodness and wisdom of our elected officials to bring our budgets into balance, because our budgets will be balanced by default.

Finally, having resolved the staying-in factor, the balancing provisions also resolve the getting-in factor: that getting into deficit spending is easier than staying out, because we make our spending-side and revenue-side policies piece-meal.

Notice what happens if we should decide, in a piece-meal fashion, to establish a new spending program or spend more money on an existing spending program. That program will assume either a new portion or an enlarged portion of the corresponding allowance—and, because of the balancing provisions, the remaining programs will assume incrementally smaller portions.

Even if we are inclined to follow our path of least resistance and make decisions about our budget in a piece-meal fashion, the balancing provisions will automatically convert those decisions into decisions about our budget as a whole. A decision impacting the priority of any one spending program will implicitly become a decision about the priority of every other spending program, too.

At the same time, although the Amendment only addresses spending-side policies, it will also impact our revenue-side policies. The Amendment does not say anything about tax policy, for example. We will be perfectly free under the Amendment to adopt whatever revenue-impacting policies we may desire. The Amendment merely requires that after we have established policies that impact our revenues, we conform our spending to fit within whatever revenues we actually receive.

So, the first balancing provision will provide guidance in establishing the discretionary and mandatory allowances. The second balancing provision will then provide guidance in fitting our desired mandatory spending within its allowance, and by example will provide guidance in fitting our desired discretionary spending within its allowance, too. In doing so, the balancing provisions resolve the getting-in factor and the staying-in factor. The first four parts of the Solvency Amendment thus resolve all three factors underlying our long-term debt problem.

There is just one catch to this solution. If the Amendment were to end here, it would effectively be making an across-the-board cut to all spending, both discretionary and mandatory. The same political resistance that would mobilize to oppose cuts in any one spending program would mobilize all the more forcefully to oppose cuts in all spending programs. Sections 1 through 4 of the Amendment do not by themselves have the sort of modest impact that we should expect a solution to our problem to have. Without more, the Amendment would never, ever pass.

This brings us to Section 5 and the final part of the Amendment.

5.5 A Harness

SECTION 5 SETS FORTH the most important part of the Solvency Amendment. It binds a resolution of the factors underlying our problem to the characteristics that we should expect a solution to have. Once the two functions of Section 5 are understood, the operation of the Amendment as a whole will become clear. It reads:

The Harness

Section 5.

After Congress has established the third allowance, and upon the beginning of the next year, Money may also be drawn from the Treasury in the next year for purposes of any and all Expenditures not under the outlay limit that Congress may subsequently and separately by law establish.

Wait...

What?

Didn't we just divide all our spending into various allowances? And then didn't we force all of our spending to fit into those allowances, in order to balance the budget? Now this Section comes along and allows Congress to spend whatever it wants beyond them! Doesn't that overturn everything else the Amendment does? Doesn't that make the Amendment totally moot?

Not at all. And this is why:

Although Sections 1 through 4 function together to resolve budget imbalances, their true role in the Solvency Amendment is not to *directly balance our budgets on their own.* Rather, their role in the Solvency Amendment is to provide a balanced-budget condition for Section 5 to use in *naturally guiding us to balance our budgets ourselves.*

Look—we are being driven toward insolvency not because deficit spending is *actually* impossible to avoid, but because it is *effectively* impossible to avoid. There is an obstacle between us and a solution to our long-term debt problem that has proven to be insurmountable: *the need for political coordination.* Ultimately, our inability to politically coordinate in order to resolve our problem has kept us spending in deficit, year after year, without any end in sight.

That obstacle has defined our path of least resistance in establishing our spending-side and revenue-side policies. As a result of that obstacle, deficits have become our default condition, *unless we can politically coordinate our way out of them.*

The first function of Section 5 is to use the balanced-budget condition provided by Sections 1 through 4 to turn that obstacle around and permanently reverse our path of least resistance. Section 5 makes balanced budgets our default condition, and permits deficits *only if we politically coordinate our way into them.*

Section 5 is the most important part of the Amendment, and one word in Section 5 is the most important word: "subsequently."

Under Section 5, we could still pass laws establishing spending beyond the outlay limit and causing a deficit in any given year. Before we could do so, however, we would have to coordinate amongst ourselves politically—and *political coordination is hard.*

What is more, to become insolvent in the long term, it would not be enough to politically coordinate our way into a deficit once. Politically coordinating once to bring the budget out of balance would only last for one year. The next year, Sections 1 through 4 would operate to re-establish a balanced-budget default condition, and we would be forced to politically coordinate again before we could bring the budget out of balance again.

In order to drive ourselves into insolvency, we would have to politically coordinate our way into deficits one year at a time, year after year, after year, after year. Perhaps under some political conditions we might be willing to do so, for a limited purpose, and for a limited time. However, those political conditions would eventually end, and upon ending, our balanced-budget default condition would step in.

Based on our history and experience, we know that weaknesses may be turned into strengths. Checks and balances between branches of government can harness the hunger for power to police the use of power. Market economies can harness self-interest to enhance the public good through the "invisible hand." In a similar vein, the Amendment harnesses the inherent difficulty of political coordination—the very thing driving us toward insolvency right now—to pull us relentlessly toward balanced budgets instead.

Faced with the need to politically coordinate in order to solve our problem, we seem as helpless as fairy-tale villagers fleeing a rampaging dragon. The Solvency Amendment seizes that dragon, breaks it to the plough, and lets it till the fields for us instead of razing them.

As the next Chapter will discuss in greater depth, with the addition of Section 5, the Amendment will erode our deficits away, and our long-term debt problem will be solved just as effectively as if our deficits had been eliminated directly. This is just as well, given the crucial second function of Section 5. As if by alchemy, Section 5 transforms the Amendment from something that could never pass into something that cannot reasonably be refused. Section 5 makes the Solvency Amendment politically achievable.

The only real reason to oppose the Amendment would be that shortfalls under the Amendment might lead to cuts in preferred spending programs. Consider, though, what would have to be true for a shortfall to lead to a cut in spending for some hypothetical Program X.

First, it would have to be true that our government's revenues were insufficient to cover all of our government's desired spending. Right from the beginning, then, spending cuts in Program X would imply that our government is attempting to live outside of its means. A shortfall would imply that our government's hands are not clean in managing its finances.

Second, it would have to be true that our government's revenues were a consequence of revenue-side policies it has established. Whatever those revenues might be, they would be due to policies—such as tax policies and regulatory policies—that we have consented to bear. So, our government would be attempting to live not just beyond its means, but beyond means resulting from the very policy decisions it has made. A shortfall would therefore also imply that our government is attempting to avoid the consequences of its own actions.

Third, it would have to be true that our government did not object to the portion of the outlay limit set aside for whichever allowance Program X falls under. If Program X were a spending program under the mandatory allowance, for example, a shortfall in funding for Program X would, in part, be due to our government's decision about how to divide the remainder of the outlay limit between the discretionary and mandatory allowances. Accordingly, a shortfall would also imply that the share of the remainder set aside for Program X's allowance reflects our government's relative priorities between discretionary and mandatory spending.

Fourth, it would have to be true that our government did not object to the portion of Program X's allowance that was set aside for Program X. Continuing the example from above, if Program X were a mandatory spending program, then a shortfall in funding for Program X would also, in part, be due to our government's decision about how much of the mandatory allowance should be devoted to Program X. So, a shortfall would also imply that Program X's share of its allowance reflects our government's relative priorities among all the various programs under that allowance.

It is also noteworthy that if Program X were a mandatory spending program, at least part of the reason for the shortfall in its funding would have been that our government was unable to politically coordinate to avoid the shortfall. Previously-sitting governments must have established appropriations binding upon the currently-sitting government that led to deficit spending, and that deficit spending must have proven to be effectively impossible for the currently-sitting government to avoid. For mandatory spending programs specifically, a shortfall would therefore also imply that previously-sitting governments must have violated the consent of the governed by saddling the currently-sitting government with deficit spending that it cannot escape to fund Program X.

In summary, for a shortfall in funding for Program X to occur, our government would have to be attempting to live beyond its means, and in the process attempting to avoid the consequences of its own actions. Additionally, Program X's funding under the Amendment would merely reflect the relative priorities our government has given first to Program X's allowance, then to Program

X within that allowance. For mandatory spending programs, the Amendment will even have reinstated appropriations for those programs right up to the maximum amount that will not risk violating the consent of the governed.

All of this would have to be true to lead to a shortfall in Program X's funding under Sections 1 through 4. With the addition of Section 5, one final thing would have to be true, too. It would have to be true that our government has declined to establish expenditures beyond the outlay limit to make up for the shortfall in Program X.

While the Amendment may lead to a shortfall in funding for Program X, it doesn't cut funding for any program by itself. Shortfalls under the Amendments only really become cuts if we allow them to. In short, the Amendment ultimately doesn't cut anything—we do.

The Amendment isolates spending that is beyond our means, and is therefore improper to begin with, then guides our remaining spending to reflect our relative priorities. If we do not restore portions of funding shortfalls in various spending programs, the resulting cuts will be the direct result of decisions made through the ordinary democratic process.

The only money that gets cut will be money that the current generation of the governed, through the currently-sitting government, does not consent to spend. But as a matter of fundamental principles, a government cannot justifiably spend money (or exercise power in any other way) without the consent of the governed. The very existence of the cut itself will prove that there is no legitimate reason to spend whatever money is being cut—at least, no reason that is legitimate in a democracy. Section 5 thus turns the only real reason to oppose the Amendment into a reason to demand it.

THE NEXT CHAPTER explores how the Amendment would change our process for establishing spending-side policies and revenue-side policies. Before beginning that discussion it would be fitting to take stock of the Amendment.

To truly solve our long-term debt problem, we must fix our process for establishing spending-side and revenue-side policies. We must do this by altering our path of least resistance, which in turn may be done by making it easier to get out of deficit spending, and by making it easier to stay out. We must also ensure that our policies do not bypass the consent of the governed.

First, the budgeting sequence, the spending conditions, and the budget constraints interact to make mandatory spending dependent upon the consent of the governed. Then the balancing provisions fit our desired spending within the allowances and make balancing our budget unavoidable, either by default mechanisms or by whatever alternate means we may provide. The addition of the balancing provisions also inescapably turns piece-meal decisions about spending into decisions about spending as a whole, and binds our spending-side decisions to our revenue-side policies. The first four parts of the Amendment thereby make getting out of deficit spending easier than staying in, and make staying out of deficit spending easier than getting in.

Moreover, although the addition of Section 5 permits deficit spending to occur, it does so only in a way that retains a balanced-budget default condition as our path of least resistance, and only in a way that is expressly dependent upon the consent of the governed. The underlying factors resolved by Sections 1 through 4 therefore remain resolved with the addition of Section 5.

The Solvency Amendment, as a whole, resolves the factors underlying our problem. However, in addition to resolving those factors, there are a number of characteristics that we should expect a solution to our problem to have.

To be able to pass, a solution to our long-term debt problem should not seek to cast blame. The solution must amend the Constitution, and to be able to do so it must be essentially unobjectionable. This could in turn be made easier if the solution were procedural in nature and if the solution were modest. Finally, it must be a complete solution to solve our problem in perpetuity.

The Solvency Amendment does not seek to cast blame. It does not blame Republicans or Democrats, liberals or conservatives, those who lean to the right or those who lean to the left, or any other group in between. It does not presume that the particular policy preferences of any one group are solely to blame for our problem and subsequently seek to punish that group by disfavoring its policy preferences. It fixes our broken process instead of trying to punish bad people.

Since it amends the Constitution, the Solvency Amendment cannot be discarded as a merely statutory solution to our problem could, and it will therefore be an enduring solution. In addition, the Amendment only provides procedures governing our spending decisions. It makes no judgments about the merits or wisdom of any particular spending policy or revenue-impacting policy. It merely provides guidance in fitting our spending-side policies within the revenues that result from our revenue-side policies, and ensures that any cuts along the way are consistent with the consent of the governed. It does not make substantive judgments about any particular policy preference.

Due to the harness presented in Section 5, the Amendment will not have any impact in and of itself. If we wish, in any given year, we could restore a shortfall in funding for any spending program—up to and including fully restoring all shortfalls in each and every spending program. As a result, the Amendment is modest, having no more impact than we consent for it to have.

Finally, the Amendment will do what it does without requiring our eternal vigilance. Once proposed and ratified, it will lead us naturally, over time, to bring our budgets into balance and keep them there all by itself. Our solvency will be nothing more than the natural outcome of establishing spending-side policies and revenue-side policies under the Amendment.

So, in addition to resolving the underlying factors, the Solvency Amendment has those characteristics that a solution to our problem should be expected to have.

The Solvency Amendment will fix our broken process for establishing spending-side and revenue-side policies and will solve our massive, intractable long-term debt problem. Sections 1 through 4 will place stark choices before us and help us to make them. Due to Section 5, however, the Amendment will not rigidly require that we make those choices, and as a result it will be inoffensive enough to actually be enacted.

The Solvency Amendment may seem to do nothing. Yet it actually does everything.

· 6 ·

THE FUTURE

ASSUME FOR A MOMENT that in some year in the future—call it Year Zero—the Solvency Amendment is proposed and ratified as required by Article V and becomes an amendment to the Constitution. The budgeting sequence would then begin in Year One, and beginning in Year Two, money could only be drawn from the Treasury in accordance with the Amendment. In every year from Year Two on, we would spend under the allowances established in the previous year while establishing the allowances for the year to come.

As things currently stand, our government is inclined to spend far more money than it receives, and deficit spending to make up the difference is our path of least resistance. The Amendment would change this. Beginning in Year Two, our discretionary spending and mandatory spending would by default be fitted to the allowances established for them, and all of our spending would by default be fitted to the amount of money we receive. If our current spending patterns are a reasonable reflection of the relative priorities that we would end up giving to our various spending programs under the Amendment, then our spending programs would face across-the-board funding shortfalls.

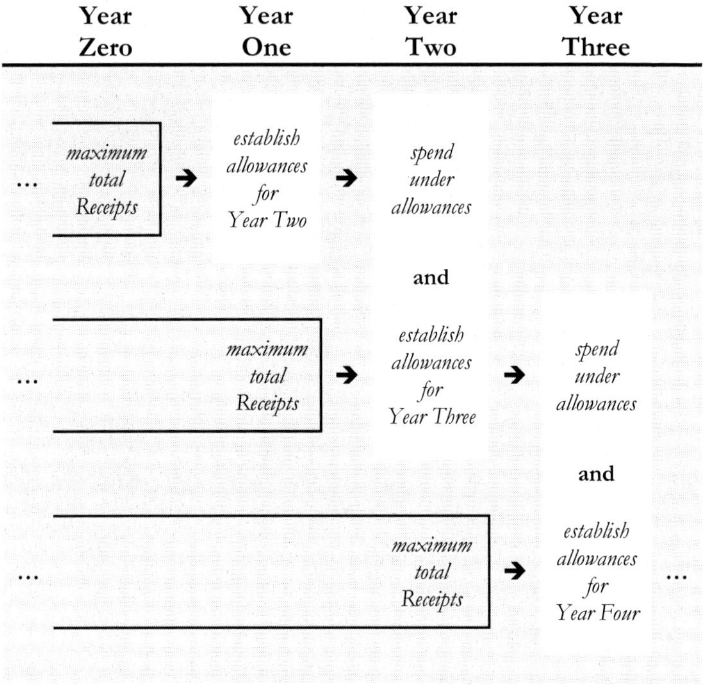

Due to the harness in Section 5, it would be possible for us to spend in deficit in order to make up for part or all of these funding shortfalls. However, since we would no longer be on autopilot, such deficit spending would not be assured, and would instead have to be secured through political coordination one year at a time.

Because of this, if we enact the Solvency Amendment it will impact our country's policies, in both the short term and the long term, in a number of ways.

6.1 Immediate Revenue-Side Debate

RIGHT FROM YEAR ZERO, the Solvency Amendment will provoke a debate about our revenue-side policies. The possibility that we may not approve deficit spending and may thereby allow our funding shortfalls to become cuts will lead to an intense push to increase our government's revenues. This would most likely take the form of an attempt to raise taxes.

There are no requirements in the Amendment regarding our revenue-side policies, including our tax policies. Any modifications to our tax policies would therefore be governed by our standard law-making process, just as they are now. Under the Amendment, we will be free to change our taxes in whichever way we might wish. The across-the-board funding shortfalls we will face beginning in Year Two will create pressure to raise our taxes in order to maintain our level of spending by increasing our revenues.

Any proposed tax increase would in turn provoke resistance for a number of reasons, beginning with the plain, self-interested desire to be taxed as little as possible. Beyond simple self-interest, it would be argued that tax increases may reduce available jobs and increase prices. It would also be argued that tax increases may reduce the rate of economic growth.

Tax increases would be resisted, in other words, for same sorts of now-familiar reasons offered in response to proposed tax increases today. Under the Amendment, though, our total outlays for spending of all types will be limited (by default, at least) to the maximum revenues received in any previous year. This means that if we were to adopt a particular change in tax policy, such as a tax increase, our future levels of spending will be affected not by the revenues that we *expect* or *forecast* or *believe* that the changes would lead to, but by the revenues that the changes *actually do* lead to.

Under the Amendment, we will still be free to establish whatever tax policies we may wish. We will have to balance out many concerns in the process, but that would be nothing new. What would be new is that we could no longer rely on automatically spending in deficit to make up for losses in expected revenues. Our spending-side policies will be bound to the consequences of our tax policies.

While our revenues are most obviously related to our tax policies, they are also related to our regulatory policies. As with tax policies, regulatory policies may impact jobs, and prices, and economic growth. As a result we will have to balance out many of the same concerns in establishing regulatory policies under the Amendment as we would in establishing tax policies—and we will be similarly bound to the consequences of our regulatory policies, too.

Any potential impact to economic growth will be of particular concern both to our tax policies and our regulatory policies. Since total outlays under the Amendment will depend upon revenues, total outlays under the Amendment over time will depend upon growth in revenues over time. Policies harming economic growth will eventually harm revenues. Therefore, even if a particular policy were to increase revenues in the short term, it may not be advisable if it also decreases revenues in the long term.

Under the Amendment, limits on our total outlays in the future will directly depend upon wise policymaking today. Any decisions that may impact revenues could no longer be made piece-meal, in isolation from other aspects of our overall fiscal picture. Instead, our spending will be bound to the actual revenues resulting from our revenue-side policies. When establishing our revenue-side policies, we will have to be ready to put our money where our mouths are, policy-wise, in a way that has never really been true before.

6.2 Immediate Spending-Side Debate

IN ADDITION TO provoking a debate about our revenue-side policies, the Solvency Amendment will directly provoke two debates about our relative priorities with respect to our spending-side policies.

We will be guided into a first debate over our relative priorities between discretionary and mandatory spending. In Year One, the budgeting sequence and the spending conditions will force us to establish the discretionary and mandatory allowances. Until we do, we will be unable to draw any money from the Treasury for purposes under them in Year Two. Meanwhile, the budget constraints will effectively reduce the establishment of both allowances to one act. After the establishment of the discretionary allowance, the mandatory allowance will be limited to whatever portion of the remainder is left over.

Although the fractions of our outlays that we currently devote to discretionary and mandatory spending would reasonably reflect our relative priorities, the Amendment will not force us to use those fractions. Instead, in Year One, we will have to debate and decide upon our relative priorities between discretionary and mandatory spending in order to establish the discretionary and mandatory allowances for Year Two.

This debate will be renewed every year. However, because of the first balancing provision, the importance of this debate will dramatically diminish after Year One.

The first balancing provision will begin to operate in Year Two. Starting in Year Two, if we cannot decide on our relative priorities between discretionary and mandatory spending by the end of the year, the allowances will by default be established to reflect the relative priorities that were established for them in the previous year.

After Year One, because of the first balancing provision, we will be guaranteed that the next year's discretionary and mandatory allowances will be in some way established. We will never have to live through a crisis in which government inaction might prevent us from drawing money from the Treasury under those allowances in the next year.

In addition to the first debate, we will be guided into a second debate over our relative priorities among the various mandatory spending programs on one hand, and over our relative priorities among the various discretionary spending programs on the other hand.

At least in the Amendment's initial years, the amount of money we will be inclined to spend under the mandatory allowance will be more than the allowance will permit. The second balancing provision will reinstate appropriations under the mandatory allowance in response to an overall shortfall in the mandatory allowance. By default, appropriations will be reinstated in one uniform proportion for all the mandatory spending programs.

Although that uniform proportion would reasonably reflect the relative priorities that we currently assign to the various mandatory spending programs, the Amendment will not force us to use that proportion. Instead, we will be free to establish alternate proportions—or any other alternate manners of reinstating our mandatory spending appropriations—so long as whatever alternate proportions or manners we establish do not violate the mandatory allowance.

Similarly, the amount of money we will be inclined to spend under the discretionary allowance will be more than the allowance will permit. Since appropriations under the discretionary allowance for the next year would not yet even exist, though, there will be nothing to proportionately reinstate.

However, the second balancing provision will provide a ready example of how spending under the discretionary allowance may be made to fit within its allowance. It will simply not be credible for advocates of the various discretionary spending programs to throw up their hands and declare "It's too hard!" or "It can't be done!" As will be obvious from the reinstatement of spending under the mandatory allowance, it can be done—if no other way can be found, then through something like the second balancing provision. Advocates of the various mandatory spending programs will be quite able to explain this if advocates of discretionary spending programs attempt to claim ignorance.

6.3 The End of Entrenched Deficit Spending

ALTHOUGH SPENDING BEYOND the outlay limit will be possible under Section 5, such deficit spending would need to be proposed and debated every year. By bringing our entrenched deficit spending to an end, the Solvency Amendment will spur policy reform on both the revenue side and the spending side.

On the revenue side, with so many spending programs facing funding shortfalls, it will be easier than ever to argue for policies to increase revenues. The immediate revenue-side debate would most likely result in a decision to increase taxes to the greatest extent that is politically possible in order to increase revenues.

On the spending side, starting in Year One, we will decide about our relative priorities between discretionary and mandatory spending as a whole, and we will also decide about our relative priorities both among the mandatory spending programs and among the discretionary spending programs.

These spending-side decisions will be made much easier in the beginning by Section 5, under which we will be free to incur deficits in support of as much spending beyond the outlay limit as we may wish. Due to political inertia, the early years would likely be a period of relative tolerance for deficit spending. Shortfalls between the spending we may desire and our budget constraints would likely be largely covered—perhaps even entirely covered—by deficit spending under Section 5.

It has become commonplace in our country for the party with the least political power to mount campaigns against deficit spending. Nobody seems to approve of deficit spending. However, nobody seems to be able to do anything about it either, and those campaigns against deficit spending seem to last just as long as it takes for the party mounting them to regain political power.

Under the Amendment, though, those campaigns will immediately gain a potency they have always lacked. People campaigning against deficit spending will no longer need to achieve a critical mass around a particular solution to our problem. Instead, they will only need to prevent a critical mass from forming around expenditures beyond the outlay limit under Section 5.

As a result, deficit spending will immediately face erosive and unrelenting political pressures. Votes in Congress for spending beyond the outlay limit will face an ever-present political resistance. These votes, like any other votes, will be subject to ordinary political wrangling and horse-trading. In particular, there will be a market in Congress to exchange these votes for political support for reforms to our revenue-side and spending-side policies in order to prevent further deficit spending.

Sooner or later, though, the period of relative tolerance for deficit spending will end. When that happens, the Amendment will prove on the back-swing to be a double-edged sword. Just as it will be easier than ever to argue for policies to increase revenues, so it will be easier than ever to argue for policies to reduce spending.

At some point, when faced with funding shortfalls in various spending programs, there will be no more room for political wrangling, and no more horses to trade. A period of relative intolerance for deficit spending will begin.

When weighing decisions to spend in deficit under Section 5 to cover significant funding shortfalls, the country will begin to say "No." When this happens, because of everything that would have to be true for the resulting cuts to occur, any arguments against the cuts will face ready and devastating counterarguments.

Funding shortfalls would imply that we are trying to live beyond our means—and by that time, we will have enacted policies to increase revenues as much as politically possible, and those policies will have had a chance to work. It will be clear, then, that any funding shortfalls signify disreputable attempts to live not just beyond our means, but beyond means that are the result of policies we have enacted.

A funding shortfall in any particular program will also be a direct result of the relative priority we have chosen to assign to that particular program. If we had wished to, we could have increased the portion of the remainder assigned to that program's allowance (whether discretionary or mandatory). Similarly, if we had wished to, we could have increased the portion of that program's allowance corresponding to that particular program. A funding shortfall would mean that we didn't think that particular program was important enough to ensure more funding for it amidst all the other programs we wish to spend money on.

Finally, if we decline to spend beyond the outlay limit to cover the funding shortfall, then we will have democratically declined to take on the deficit spending that would have eliminated the shortfall. We will have thereby proven to ourselves that the governed did not consent to that deficit spending—making that deficit spending an unjust exercise of power, and making the corresponding cuts entirely proper.

Even after we have proven this to ourselves, cuts in funding for mandatory spending programs in particular may be characterized in morally-charged terms as a type of faithlessness. It has become commonplace to hear various mandatory spending programs referred to as "promises" that we have made as a country to various of our citizens. Should funding for mandatory spending programs be cut, it will be said that we are breaking our promises.

However, we will have proven to ourselves by the very operation of the Amendment that whatever deficit spending we may end up declining does not have the consent of the governed. For this reason, should we decline to spend in deficit to cover funding shortfalls in our mandatory spending programs, we will have proven something else to ourselves, too.

We will have proven that whatever mandatory spending may be cut is spending that could not satisfy the basic requirements of democratic legitimacy. So, if mandatory spending programs are thought of as promises, then whatever cuts we may end up making to them under the Amendment would represent promises that should never have been made, and should never have been believed.

The tragic truth of our situation is that over time our revenue-side and spending-side policies have come to foster contradictory expectations. If we are to deal with our deficit spending, we cannot hope to satisfy all of those contradictory expectations. That is just not going to be possible.

We have known for a very long time now that we would face a reckoning over our deficit spending and our growing debt. We have often bemoaned the burden we were placing on the future and on our children. Well, that future is now. We are those children, and our reckoning has arrived.

We are absolutely going to fail to live up to all of the contradictory expectations we have accumulated over time—including, potentially, those expectations that seem like promises. Our task cannot be to meet all of our expectations. Our task must instead be, in the course of failing to meet all of our expectations, to fail as gracefully as possible.

Some say we have a revenue problem, and some say we have a spending problem. While there is some truth to both perspectives, our real problem is a *reconciliation* problem. Our problem is our seeming inability to establish revenue-side policies with an eye toward the amount of spending we'd like, and then reconcile our spending-side policies to live within whatever revenues may result.

There is no good way to go from our deficit spending to this reconciliation. Instead of holding out for a good way, we must steel ourselves to search for the least-bad way. Through the course of ordinary political debate under the Solvency Amendment, the least-bad way to this reconciliation is exactly what we will find.

6.4 A Poison Drawn Out

OUR ENTRENCHED DEFICIT SPENDING has fostered poisonous illusions about the sorts of policies that are politically achievable. It is easier to advocate a preferred spending-side or revenue-side policy when deficit spending will automatically cover any funding shortfalls that the policy might cause. It is easier, for example, to advocate more spending when that spending is not made conditional upon higher revenues. Similarly, it is easier to advocate lower taxes when future spending is not made conditional upon whatever revenues may follow the tax cut.

Our piece-meal consideration of policies allows each side of the political spectrum to enact, from time to time, scraps of the policy vision it favors. Seeing those scraps enacted, each side comes to operate under illusions about the achievability of its entire policy vision.

The Solvency Amendment will dispel these poisonous illusions. Once piece-meal policy evaluation has ended, deficit spending will no longer be the background assumption. We will no longer be able to avoid conflict and hide from hard choices. We will instead have to consider the spending side of our policies and the revenue side of our policies together and will be guided to reconcile the two. Any deficit spending will have to be driven by the force of argument instead of merely the force of inertia.

This would likely make it harder for each side of the political spectrum to enact portions of its policy vision. Each side may even find that it would have to give up portions of its policy vision that have already been enacted. This will simply reflect the true amount of political support for those policy visions that will exist when we are forced to confront the tensions among our desired policies, engage in the conflicts we have been avoiding, and reconcile our spending-side and revenue-side policies with each other.

Since the political limits of various policies will be made clearer to us, political rhetoric regarding policies that impact our budget will not get as far on one-dimensional characterizations driven by blind partisanship. Our rhetoric will have to accommodate itself better to political realities.

Calls for changes in our policies will, out of necessity, have to become more reasoned and thoughtful. Instead of endless moans for *"more!"* in our debates, we will begin to hear things like *"more than,"* and *"because."* Having eliminated piece-meal policy making, we will finally force ourselves to treat public money as the scarce resource it actually is.

6.5 Better Revenue-Side Policies

THE REVENUE-SIDE DEBATE that will begin in Year Zero will continue in Year One and beyond. The security of funding for our spending-side policies in future years will become directly dependent upon the wisdom of our revenue-side policies. Advocates of spending programs will be led to take a direct interest in the actual consequences of policies that impact revenues, such as our tax policies and our regulatory policies.

This will lead to an attitudinal reform toward revenue-impacting policies. All new laws dealing with taxation and regulation will be seriously scrutinized for their potential impact upon future revenues. A reckless disregard for the impact of various policies upon revenues will not be possible. Having to bear the actual consequences of our revenue-side policies will guide our government to become a more thoughtful caretaker for our economy. This will lead to better revenue-side policies in the fullness of time.

6.6 Better Spending-Side Policies

ON THE SPENDING SIDE, the two debates provoked by the Amendment will also continue. From Year Two onward, the Amendment's balancing provisions will prompt us to determine whether we want to adjust the relative priorities we assign to discretionary and mandatory spending as a whole. The balancing provisions will also prompt us to consider the relative priorities we assign to the various discretionary spending programs and the relative priorities we assign to the various mandatory spending programs.

It will still be possible for Congress to establish appropriations for future years, or to increase previously-established appropriations for future years. The Amendment will just change the significance of those appropriations. By default, the second balancing provision will turn an increase in funding for a particular mandatory spending program into an increase in the proportion of the mandatory allowance spent for that program—and a corresponding decrease in the proportion spent for all other programs. If more of the mandatory allowance is spent on one program, then less will be spent on each of the others.

The balancing provisions will thereby inescapably turn piecemeal decisions about spending on any one program into decisions about spending on all programs. In effect, new appropriations of specific amounts of money in future years will be changed into appropriations of shares of the mandatory allowance, and adding new shares will just dilute any shares that already exist.

This will in turn place the various spending programs in competition with each other for the affection of the citizenry. Money spent on each spending program will come to be intensely scrutinized by advocates of the other spending programs, for waste as well as simple inefficiency. Any waste or inefficiency in a spending program will be seen as shares of spending that can in good conscience be withheld from that program—for example, by reducing the proportional reinstatement of that program's appropriations. Each spending program will therefore have an incentive to make the best possible use of the money given to it.

It has become commonplace to hear various spending programs referred to as "investments." While this characterization is not baseless, it does not lend itself to the thoughtful allocation of public money. After all, investments can be good, but they can also be bad. To the extent that our spending programs may be considered investments, the competition for our affection will lead us to focus on the returns on our investments—i.e., the actual results of our spending.

The Amendment will therefore also lead to an attitudinal reform toward spending policies. Our spending programs will have systemic incentives to become as efficient as possible. Over time, this will lead to better spending-side policies, too.

6.7 The Beginning of Something New

A GREAT MANY THINGS divide us from one another in the political life of our country. Much of what divides us involves our spending and revenue-impacting policies: taxes, regulations, the sorts of things we should spend money on, and how much money we should spend.

Our process for establishing our spending-side and revenue-side policies is broken, though. Trying to find common ground over those policies is hard enough by itself. Having to work within a broken process makes finding common ground even harder.

The Amendment will fix that broken process, and in the course of doing so will guide us to reconcile our spending to the size of our revenue stream. Our spending will come to be driven by our ability to pay rather than by our appetites.

In shaping our policies, the Amendment will not pick winners and losers. Debates over our spending-side and revenue-side policies present the sorts of questions that the people within a democracy must answer for themselves. The Amendment will require that we pick winners and losers ourselves, but will prevent us from using deficit spending as a means of conflict avoidance in the process.

The Amendment itself is utterly disinterested in which side of the political spectrum wins any of our political wrestling matches. It will merely require that we hold our wrestling matches and live with the results.

We may still choose to be fiscally foolish. We can hardly be a free people, after all, if we are not free to make mistakes. But becoming insolvent won't be easy. If we become insolvent, it will be because we have dragged ourselves into insolvency: bit by bit, reaching and clawing, pulling and straining, spitting and screaming, every bloody inch of the way.

While insolvency will always be a hypothetical possibility for us, it will never again be an existential fear. There will be no more hand-wringing crises over our debt problem, no more brink-of-disaster moments. We will no longer need to rely upon our elected officials to perform superhuman feats of political forbearance and wisdom to pull us out of the mess we are in. Getting out of our deficit spending will instead be our path of least resistance, and we will only have to guard against slipping back in.

If we can muster the resolve to put the Amendment in place, we will balance our budgets ourselves in the natural course of events. Our elections will determine the exact shape of the policies we will adopt to balance our budgets, but one way or another, those policies will come.

Over time we will find the least-bad way to reconcile our spending to our revenues. In doing so we will discover as a country which policies we care least about and which policies we care most about, through the relative priorities that we end up democratically placing upon them.

The Solvency Amendment may do more than solve our debt problem, though. As a bank account may benefit from compound interest, the continuous debates that the Amendment provokes over our revenue-side and spending-side policies may have cumulative benefits that would guide our government to become something we have not yet seen before.

Having been placed in competition with each other for our affection, our spending programs will have new incentives to provide maximum return on investment and to police themselves for waste, fraud, and abuse. Just as competitive forces drive firms in an economy to improve themselves, competitive forces introduced by the Amendment will drive our spending programs to improve themselves, too.

We might not expect the benefits of that competition to accrue in only a year, or two, or five. However, in the long term—in ten, twenty-five, or fifty years—competitive forces are likely to forge spending programs whose impact and efficiency are much greater than we have become accustomed to.

In addition to competition among our spending programs, another motivating force may also have a cumulative benefit under the Amendment. We are currently motivated to establish policies and programs in order to impact our country in lasting ways. In general, we want to improve our country, and to leave it a better place for the next generation. There are certainly differences among ourselves over what would be "better" for us as a country, but this impulse seems to be universal: We want to establish policies that can serve as a legacy for future generations.

Under the Amendment, however, the resources devoted to any particular spending program will depend upon the relative priority that future governments choose to assign to it. If programs are established with costs that would explode in future years, for example, the Amendment will scale back those costs by default. Each future government will then have to politically coordinate—one year at a time—in order to re-establish some or all of the program's funding through deficit spending, or to increase the relative priority it assigns to that program's funding.

As a result of the Amendment, the extent to which any policy may serve as a legacy for future generations will come to depend upon the extent to which future generations wish to enforce levels of spending established for that policy by previous generations. The Amendment will tend to make legacies fragile and subject to how programs are handled by future generations of the governed.

There will be at least one way for a currently-sitting government to ensure that any program it establishes could become a lasting legacy, though. A program could be designed not to spend set amounts of money, but to adjust the way in which it spends the money given to it in response to how much money it is given.

If a program designed to respond to changes in funding was given a relatively high amount of money, then it would spend the money given to it in whatever way has been established for it to spend that amount of money. If a responsive spending program was given a relatively low amount of money, though, it would do exactly the same thing—spend the money given to it whatever way has been established for it to spend that amount of money.

For a responsive spending program, the amount of money a future government may wish to spend on that program will not affect the nature of the program itself. That program's legacy—the way in which it makes use of the money given to it, whatever that amount may be—will endure.

A tumbleweed may prove to be more durable than a mighty tree by giving way before the wind. Programs designed to respond to changes in spending priorities will similarly be more durable under the Amendment than programs that rely upon the spending priorities of future governments. The legacy of a responsive spending program will survive intact, regardless of how much money future governments may wish to give it.

Modifying our spending programs to be responsive would be sensible. From the outset, the goal of living within our means requires that our spending does not exceed our revenues. However, while we have direct control over our spending, our control over our revenues is indirect at best. By its very nature, the act of balancing our budgets must make our spending conditional upon our revenues. To make spending programs explicitly responsive to our revenues would merely embed within our spending programs the conditionality that any effort to balance our budgets would require.

More importantly, while a relatively low level of funding might prevent a responsive spending program from doing as much as it otherwise might, it will not break the program. A responsive spending program will just do as much as it could with whatever it has. Funding shortfalls would simply not be possible for such a program: It will be solvent at an individual level no matter how much money is given to it.

Under the Amendment, our impulse to establish lasting legacies will provide an incentive for us to structure our spending programs to be responsive to the money that is given to them to spend. And if this motivating force led to a general movement over time toward responsive spending programs, the result would be extraordinary.

If our government were formed from the bottom up out of programs that were individually solvent, then our national budgetary debates could be reduced to establishing our relative priorities. We would only need to determine our relative priorities among our various spending programs, and each program could then be allocated a corresponding fraction of our total outlays. Being responsive, each program would then spend its fraction of our outlays in the best way it could.

The primary motivation for us to spend in deficit now is to avoid funding shortfalls in our various spending programs. If our government's programs were each solvent individually, then no matter what our total revenues may be, our primary motivation to spend in deficit would cease to exist. The entire structure of American government would become inherently solvent.

Under the Amendment, bit by bit, we will make individual decisions not to cover shortfalls in spending for our various programs. We will make decisions about our relative spending priorities that are shaped by competitive forces. Our desire to leave lasting legacies will provide a motivation for us to reform our programs to be responsive to their levels of funding.

In making our policy choices we will chip away at the structure of our government, like a sculptor chipping away at a block of marble. When we are done we will be left with a country with no long-term debt problem, whose finances are structurally sound, a country which will be able to temporarily spend in deficit to face challenges that may arise and will be guided to end that deficit spending naturally as those challenges subside.

Our choices will reveal a government that is both more effective and more resilient. We may even find that we have sculpted something that can be described with words we do not normally use in describing government. We may find ourselves with something elegant; something dynamic; something whose fit silhouette we can, from our vantage point in the present, only glancingly envision: something wonderful.

6.8 One Dividend More

THE SOLVENCY AMENDMENT WILL fix our broken process for establishing revenue-side and spending-side policies. But that process is not the only thing broken in American government.

Today, in this country, we are suffering from an infection. This infection is serious.

As if out of an apocalyptic horror film, some people among us seem to have turned into vampires, horrible evil beings plotting and scheming to dominate, control, and parasitically use the masses. Many others seem to have turned into zombies, a horrible evil horde mindlessly following and carrying out the destructive orders of its vampire masters. Fortunately, as if out of some science fiction or fantasy epic, a band of brave rebels has stepped forward to thwart the vampires and their evil schemes. These rebels have rallied a valiant resistance movement in order to defeat the zombie horde.

Under our infection, though, we can't seem to agree on who among us are the vampires and zombies, and who are the rebel leaders and the resistance. We're pretty clear on the two sides. We know that it's a matter of good versus evil, with the country's future hanging in the balance. It's just that each side keeps pointing at the other and shouting "Vampires! Zombies!"

This country is suffering from excessive partisanship. Reasonable people who disagree are funneled into an unreasoning hatred of each other. Each side of the political spectrum is encouraged to view the other as crazy, or stupid, or evil, or some combination of the three.

On one hand, political differences are to some extent unavoidable, and given all the principles and policies involved the stakes are indeed very high. Since we are trying to balance various principles that are inherently in tension with each other, political tensions of some degree are necessary, and even healthy. On the other hand, our bitter partisanship far exceeds what is healthy or inevitable. Excessive partisanship has broken our political culture.

We are not enemies. We are all Americans, every one of us. We are fellow citizens and neighbors. We are family. We are friends. In our better moments we remember this. In the day-to-day course of political life in our country, though, this seems to be amazingly hard for us to keep in mind.

Maybe that other guy isn't irrational, or foolish, or bad. Maybe that other guy just has his own perspective on the world, coming from his own experience within it, an experience that is no less valid merely because it is different. Maybe in resolving the inherent tensions between our various principles and ideals, his judgment just reflects his own valid experience. Certainly, in a democracy, no one person's judgment is inherently privileged over anybody else's.

In defending our fundamental principles, though, we notice when judgments expressed by others are consistent with our own, and when they seem to conflict. Judgments in line with our own nurture trust. Judgments at odds with our own nurture mistrust. When considering various issues of the day, we then tune out people whose judgment we have come to mistrust. Partisanship both fuels and feeds off of this ideological self-sorting.

This self-sorting is all natural, understandable, and perhaps even beneficial to some degree, but it can become an obstacle to rational discussion and thought. It is a logical fallacy to reason from authority: Just because somebody says a thing is so, does not make it so. However, the danger of falsely reasoning from authority is present whenever we divide ourselves from each other along ideological lines.

At least some judgments expressed by people at opposite ends of the political spectrum depend upon the poisonous illusions that are caused by our current broken process for establishing our spending-side and revenue-side policies. According to some of those judgments, for example, all of our troubles are because we won't raise taxes enough to cover our level of spending (or, alternatively, because we won't cut spending to match our level of revenues). If only we would raise our taxes high enough (or cut our spending low enough), all of our problems would be solved!

The Solvency Amendment will help partisans on each side of the political spectrum to see that neither side's policy vision is entirely possible, and that judgments based on fully enacting either policy vision are therefore not realistic. The Amendment will lead each side of the political spectrum away from judgments based upon those poisonous illusions.

It has become commonplace to hear intense frustration with our excessive partisanship. It has also become commonplace to hear promises to resolve our excessive partisanship—promises that somehow seem to keep falling by the way-side.

Our excessive partisanship has many sources. By dispelling our poisonous illusions, the Amendment will eliminate at least one of those sources and will thereby improve our political culture. Such an improvement would admittedly be modest, but it would at least have the benefit of being real.

The Solvency Amendment will head off unrealistic judgments about political realities and prevent them from nurturing mistrust in others. As a result, when defending our fundamental principles, we may find ourselves open to considering the judgments of a wider range of people than we otherwise would. Once our poisonous illusions have been dispelled and we have reconciled our revenue-side and spending-side policies, we may find that we are not as divided over those policies as we now seem to be.

And while those policies are much of what divides us from one another in the political life of our country, there are other policies that also divide us. If we can bring ourselves to extend a wary hand across the aisle over our revenue-side and spending-side policies, perhaps we will find enough common ground to help us face the other policies that divide us, too.

THE SOLVENCY AMENDMENT WILL SOLVE our long-term debt problem. Having done that, by improving our political culture, it will also help us resolve whatever other problems we may have. In this way, with a single constitutional amendment, we can permanently fix much of what is broken in American government.

· 7 ·
Now

To be, or not to be—that is the question:
Whether 'tis nobler in the mind to suffer
The slings and arrows of outrageous fortune
Or to take arms against a sea of troubles,
And by opposing end them.
– Shakespeare, *Hamlet*

CURRENTLY, EACH YEAR, our country spends in deficit by default unless and until the House of Representatives, the Senate, and the President can coordinate among themselves politically to establish a balanced budget. Under the Solvency Amendment, our country would instead start each year with a balanced budget by default, unless and until we politically coordinate our way into deficits. We know that the presumption of innocence in criminal trials serves as a safeguard of justice. Similarly, by ensuring that our budgets are balanced by default, the Amendment would safeguard American solvency.

Perhaps you have been convinced that the Solvency Amendment would be good for us to consider as a country. Perhaps you are wondering how the Amendment could be made a reality.

Two things would have to be done to enact the Solvency Amendment. In reverse order, the second thing that must be done is to undertake the two-step proposal-and-ratification process for amending the Constitution. That process will be very involved and complicated. However, we will only need to deal with it later. Whatever details may need to be sorted out can safely be sorted out once the time is right to propose the Amendment.

The first thing that must to be done, then, is to make the time right to propose the Amendment. Fortunately, the process for doing that is straightforward, with just one easy step: *Spread the word.*

Spread the word about the Solvency Amendment. Talk about it with your family. Talk about it with your friends. Talk about it with your representatives and senators, both at the State level and the Federal level. Tell everybody you can about it, and encourage them to talk about it, too.

Our country is in danger, but we can defend it. We can disengage our autopilot and bring our entrenched deficit spending to an end. If we can rouse ourselves to make this one Amendment we can solve our long-term debt problem once and for all. Then—having once more secured the blessings of our liberty—we can return in good conscience to a more innocent citizenship.

As the saying goes, the journey of a thousand miles begins with one step. The journey toward American solvency will require a constitutional amendment. But as long and as hard as that journey may be, it can begin with one simple question:

Have you heard about the Solvency Amendment?

APPENDIX: SUMMARY

AMERICAN SOLVENCY

CURRENTLY, EACH YEAR, our country spends in deficit by default unless and until the House of Representatives, the Senate, and the President can coordinate among themselves politically to establish a balanced budget. Under the Solvency Amendment, our country would instead start each year with a balanced budget by default, unless and until we politically coordinate our way into deficits. We know that the presumption of innocence in criminal trials serves as a safeguard of justice. Similarly, by ensuring that our budgets are balanced by default, the Amendment would safeguard American solvency.

1. In Brief

AMERICA HAS a long-term debt problem. Our government continually spends far more money than it receives. The deficit between the two is financed by taking out debt. That debt accumulates, and if it gets so large that we cannot service it, America will become insolvent.

The cause of our problem is easy to understand. Water flows downhill, following the path of least resistance. Societies tend to follow paths of least resistance, too. To stay out of deficit spending, or to get out of deficit spending, the House of Representatives, the Senate, and the President would have to coordinate among themselves politically. Such political coordination is hard, though, and as a result we regularly spend in deficit despite our best intentions. Deficit spending is just our path of least resistance.

The Solvency Amendment will solve our long-term debt problem. The Amendment has five parts.

The first four parts would balance our budget for us in a default manner each year, while allowing us to freely substitute that default balanced-budget for whatever other manner of balancing our budgets may be more to our liking. Then, having established a default balanced budget for the year, the fifth part would allow us to pass laws to spend whatever we may wish to beyond that.

Although the fifth part may seem to cancel out the rest of the Amendment, it is actually the Amendment's most important part. The fifth part has two crucial functions.

First, by making us pass new laws each and every year before we can spend in deficit, the Amendment permanently reverses our path of least resistance. Deficits are currently our default condition *unless we can politically coordinate our way out of them.* The Amendment balances our budgets by default, and permits deficits *only if we politically coordinate our way into them.* So, the obstacle that is currently preventing us from balancing our budgets—the difficulty of coordinating among ourselves politically—becomes an obstacle preventing us from spending in deficit, instead.

Second, by permitting whatever deficit spending we can politically coordinate to enact in a given year, the Amendment ensures that it isn't making any spending cuts itself in the course of balancing the budget. If there is a shortfall in the amount of money we'd like to spend on any program, we will be able to spend that money by passing a new law to approve it. In other words, the Amendment ultimately won't be making any cuts—we will.

By naturally guiding us to balance our budgets ourselves, the Amendment will solve our long-term debt problem. By ensuring that we are ultimately the ones making spending cuts, the Amendment becomes politically achievable.

2. In Detail

THERE ARE ***three factors*** underlying our long-term debt problem. The first factor is that when considering various potential revenue-side and spending-side policies, we could either keep our overall finances in mind, or we could consider those policies piece-meal. We end up considering policies piece-meal because it is the path of least resistance: *it is easier for us to get into deficit spending than it is for us to stay out.*

The second factor is that after we begin spending in deficit, we could either balance our budgets, or we could avoid balancing them and continue our deficits. We end up not balancing our budgets and instead continue our deficit spending because it is the path of least resistance: *it is easier for us to stay in deficit spending than it is for us to get out.*

Under the first two factors, our deficit spending has occurred simply because in the course of establishing our spending-side and revenue-side policies, we have followed our path of least resistance. However, there is a third factor hiding in the interaction between the first two, one far more troubling.

Previous generations of Americans established a full range of mandatory spending programs. However, because those programs were established piece-meal, minimal consideration was given to whether their cumulative burdens would be financially feasible, which has helped to bring about our deficit spending. Then, because balancing our budgets is inherently difficult, we have been unable to bring an end to our deficit spending.

Despite our clear desire to stop spending in deficit, it has proven to be effectively impossible for us to politically coordinate to do so. Previous generations have thus committed the current generation to reckless deficit spending that we cannot avoid. The third factor is that *the policies causing our deficit spending are not even democratically legitimate, because they effectively violate the consent of the governed.*

IN ORDER TO SOLVE our long-term debt problem, we must resolve these underlying factors. A solution cannot end there, however, because there are also ***a number of characteristics*** that we should expect a solution to have.

A solution will have to be *a constitutional amendment*, which in turn means that it will have to be essentially *unobjectionable*. To make the solution most feasible, it should be *procedural* in nature. Similarly, it should strive to be *modest* in scope, despite necessarily having far-reaching consequences. Finally, a solution must be *complete*, and should not require eternal vigilance on the part of future generations.

THE SOLVENCY AMENDMENT RESOLVES the factors underlying our long-term debt problem while also having the characteristics that we should expect a solution to have.

The Amendment has ***five interlocking parts*** implemented across five Sections. The first four parts, whose implementation is spread out over Sections 1 through 4, are a budgeting sequence, spending conditions, budget constraints, and two balancing provisions.

The *budgeting sequence* requires that four budgetary amounts be established every year, one after the other: an *outlay limit*, an *interest allowance* for unavoidable spending (such as interest payments for servicing the public debts), a *discretionary allowance* for avoidable discretionary spending, and a *mandatory allowance* for avoidable mandatory spending.

The *spending conditions* prevent money from being spent under each of the three allowances until each allowance has been established. Once an allowance has been established, money may then be spent under that allowance, but only up to the limit of that allowance.

The *budget constraints* limit each of the four budgetary amounts. Under one constraint, the outlay limit cannot exceed the maximum revenue of any previous year, and the interest allowance must be sufficient to cover unavoidable spending. Under another constraint, the discretionary and mandatory allowances cannot, when combined, exceed the *remainder* of the outlay limit after the interest allowance has been removed.

The *first balancing provision* requires that, unless we say otherwise, the discretionary allowance will be the same fraction of the remainder that it was the previous year. The first balancing provision thus ensures that both the discretionary and mandatory allowances will be reasonable default proportions of the remainder while allowing us to establish them in whatever alternate proportions we may prefer.

The mandatory allowance is likely to be only a fraction of the total money required to cover the mandatory spending to which we have been committed. So, the *second balancing provision* requires that, unless we say otherwise, whatever mandatory spending we have been committed to is reinstated in that same fraction. If there is a shortfall between the mandatory spending to which we are committed and the mandatory allowance, then unless we say otherwise that shortfall will by default be distributed in an across-the-board manner to all mandatory spending. The second balancing provision ensures that shortfalls in funding under the mandatory allowance will be distributed in a reasonable manner while allowing us to distribute those shortfalls in whatever alternate manner we may prefer.

The four parts implemented in Sections 1 through 4 of the Amendment have two properties. The first property is that they resolve the factors underlying our long-term debt problem. They make our spending commitments conditional upon the consent of the governed. They balance our budgets and inescapably convert piece-meal decisions about spending into decisions about spending as a whole, making it easier for us to get out of deficit spending, and to stay out.

Without more, however, the first four parts of the Amendment would tend to implement across-the-board cuts in all of our spending in the course of balancing our budgets. The second property of the first four parts is that they are not politically achievable.

Section 5 implements the fifth and final part of the amendment: *a harness.* Once Sections 1 through 4 have established a default balanced-budget condition, Section 5 permits deficit spending, but only if we politically coordinate in that year to pass laws establishing that spending—and political coordination is hard. To drive ourselves into insolvency, we would have to politically coordinate over and over and over again. Sooner or later, we would be unable to do so, and our default balanced-budget condition would remain.

The harness thus has two functions. The first function is that it allows us to break the balanced-budget default condition established by the first four parts of the Amendment, but only in a way that places deficit spending on our path of least resistance, and only in a way that expressly depends upon the consent of the governed. The underlying factors resolved by Sections 1 through 4 therefore remain resolved with the addition of Section 5.

The second and critical function of the harness is that it makes the Solvency Amendment politically achievable.

The only reason to oppose the Amendment would be that it might cut spending. However, while the Amendment may lead to shortfalls in funding for various spending programs, Section 5 will permit us to restore funding shortfalls—up to and including fully restoring all funding shortfalls in each and every spending program.

This means that any shortfalls caused by the Amendment will only mature into cuts if we allow them to. The Amendment ultimately doesn't cut anything—under the Amendment, by declining to spend in deficit to cover shortfalls in spending, we make the cuts ourselves. Moreover, the very process by which we arrive at the cuts will prove to us that whatever spending is cut is spending that is not democratically legitimate.

The Solvency Amendment will resolve the factors underlying our long-term debt problem, and in doing so it will fix our broken process for establishing revenue-side and spending-side policies. The Solvency Amendment is thus a solution to our long-term debt problem.

THAT PROCESS IS NOT the only aspect of American government that is broken, though. This country suffers from an excessive partisanship that fosters among our citizens an unwarranted mistrust of each other. That excessive partisanship has broken our political culture.

In the course of fixing our process for establishing spending-side and revenue-side policies, the Amendment will also dispel some poisonous illusions that are a side effect of that broken process. By dispelling those poisonous illusions, the Amendment will eliminate one cause of our excessive partisanship, which will improve our political culture.

THE SOLVENCY AMENDMENT WILL SOLVE our long-term debt problem. Having done that, by improving our political culture, it will also help us resolve whatever other problems we may have. In this way, with a single constitutional amendment, we can permanently fix much of what is broken in American government.

The Solvency Amendment

Section 1. The outlay limit

Money shall not be drawn from the Treasury in the next year except in accordance with this Amendment and under this Constitution.

Every year, after the beginning of its first assembly, Congress shall by law establish an outlay limit for the next year.

The outlay limit shall not exceed the maximum total Receipts of public Money from Taxes, Duties, Imposts, and Excises in any previous year.

Section 2. The first allowance [the interest allowance]

After establishing the outlay limit, Congress shall by law establish a first allowance of the outlay limit, which shall be for the purposes of Expenditures in the next year that are not avoidable by law, to include the costs of servicing the public Debts.

The first allowance shall be sufficient to satisfy the purposes under the first allowance; and any part of the outlay limit in excess of the first allowance shall be the remainder of the outlay limit.

Upon establishing the first allowance, Money may be drawn from the Treasury in the next year for purposes under the first allowance, up to the limit of the first allowance.

Section 3. The second allowance [the discretionary allowance]

After establishing the first allowance, Congress shall by law establish a second allowance of the outlay limit, which shall be for the purposes of any amounts that Congress may reserve for Expenditures in the next year under Appropriations to be made in the next year.

Unless Congress establishes the second allowance otherwise before the beginning of the next year, the second allowance shall be established so that the Proportion which it shall bear to any remainder is equal to the Proportion which the previously-established second allowance shall have born to the previous remainder.

Upon establishing the second allowance, Money may also be drawn from the Treasury in the next year for purposes under the second allowance, up to the limit of the second allowance.

Section 4. The third allowance [the mandatory allowance]

After establishing the second allowance, Congress shall by law establish a third allowance of the outlay limit, which shall be for the purposes of Expenditures in the next year under Appropriations made before the next year that are avoidable by law.

The sum of the second allowance and the third allowance shall not exceed any remainder.

Congress shall determine the amount sufficient to satisfy the purposes under the third allowance, and if that amount should exceed the third allowance, any and all Appropriations of Money in the next year for each such purpose shall be reinstated in the Proportion which the third allowance shall bear to that amount.

Congress may by law provide for alternate reinstatement Proportions or other manners of reinstating Appropriations of Money for purposes under the third allowance; but no such provision shall be valid unless the combination of all such provisions does not violate the third allowance.

Upon establishing the third allowance, Money may also be drawn from the Treasury in the next year for purposes under the third allowance, up to the limit of the third allowance.

Section 5.

After Congress has established the third allowance, and upon the beginning of the next year, Money may also be drawn from the Treasury in the next year for purposes of any and all Expenditures not under the outlay limit that Congress may subsequently and separately by law establish.

ACKNOWLEDGEMENTS

Many thanks to my wife Pam for all of her advice and support. Many thanks as well to my friends Chris Storey and Geoff Gustafson, whose talents improved this work from conception to completion. All flaws herein are mine and mine alone; that being said, if not for Pam, and if not for Geoff and Chris, this book would not exist.

Thanks to Andy Ly for providing valuable advice and perspective. Thanks as well to Thom Blair for his editorial assistance.

Made in United States
North Haven, CT
04 November 2026

21771759R00072